What My Suicide Attempt Taught Me
About God and Living Life to the Fullest

SAM EATON

Paperback: ISBN 978-1-7355854-6-8
Ebook: ISBN 978-1-7355854-0-6
Library of Congress Number: 2020916655
First Edition: November 2020
Edited by Beth Saadati
Cover art by Grace Bennett, Creative Edge
Layout by Grace Bennett, Creative Edge

I have tried to re–create events, locales, and conversations from my memories of them. In order to maintain their anonymity, in some instances I have changed the names of individuals and places, as well as some identifying characteristics and details such as dates, physical properties, occupations, and places of residence.

Printed in the United States of America.

To Jenna Saadati & Andrew Wedekind
Forever loved and never forgotten

CONTENTS

AUTHOR'S NOTE

Dear friend,

This is my journey from suicide attempt toward abundant life. I share it with you in hopes that you can see yourself or someone you love in my story and find the courage to start conversations about faith, mental health, depression, and suicide. Waiting for you in the pages ahead are my stories of struggle and failure, how I won my life back, what my suicide attempt taught me about the real heart of God, and my ongoing struggle to live with all my might.

I am not a pastor, a deep-sea diver, an Avenger, or a mongoose whisperer. I have never sawed off my own arm, had my hand digested by a shark, or experienced any other amazing feat of humanity. I am just an average guy who found his world slipping away and—in a moment of extreme clarity—made the terrifying decision to stay and chase a life that is fully and recklessly alive.

Care to come along? I'll share my popcorn.

In this together,
Sam Eaton

PART ONE

CHAPTER 1

YOU CAN FIND YOUR PURPOSE

AGE 23

I HAD BEEN DREAMING of this moment all day: to be completely alone with the darkness within me. Who would ever have imagined simply being alive could hurt this much? After years of barely hanging on, suicide—my only solution to stop the unbearable pain—had become my brain's greatest obsession. In front of the bathroom mirror at work, I scrunched my face and imagined a gun firing against my temple. On long walks, I lingered on the Stone Arch Bridge in downtown Minneapolis and imagined a quick jump overboard into the treacherous rapids below. During lonely drives, I stared into passing high beams and imagined a sharp, deadly swerve into oncoming traffic.

A few weeks prior, I gave myself a dangerous ultimatum. On Christmas Day I would either end my life or never think about suicide again. Both passive and active suicidal thoughts had moved in and out of my consciousness for the better part of ten years. Now, at the age of twenty-three, enough was enough. It was the time to end it so everyone could get on with their lives without the burden of my moody and worthless existence.

With only six days until Christmas, I threw off my navy-checkered dress shirt, the one every business casual man owns to convince the world he cares slightly more about the way he looks than the average caveman, but not so much that he might be perceived as "fashion forward." I plopped down into my black-leather executive chair with a rush of energy that sprang up unexpectedly despite my elementary teacher exhaustion. Time to get down to business.

The night before, while fighting the magnetic pull of the knife hidden in my dresser, I started writing my suicide goodbye letters. My past trauma wafted through my childhood bedroom like someone had been chain-smoking for forty years with the windows closed. My six-foot-three-inch frame was merely a clown suit hiding the unhealed boy within me.

Opening my laptop, I felt drunk with power deciding who deserved a letter and whom I could offensively omit. For a few of the notes, my fingers flew across the keyboard as if my phalanges had been waiting years for the sentences to be released into the atmosphere. For others, a blinking cursor haunted me and produced a stream of tears at the thought of never speaking to my friends again. I imagined the betrayal they would feel to have spent so much time with me only to find out I never shared the tornado of pain within.

After a few hours, my phone vibrated against the cheap, cracked surface of my some-assembly-required plywood desk. I was late. The annual Christmas outing with my mom, sister, and sister's boyfriend aroused zero excitement. I weighed my options: call in sick and fight the backlash or perform the "everything's fine" role I had mastered all too well. As the end of my life grew closer, I was finding it almost impossible to get into that character, and I had less desire than ever to be around anyone who might figure out what I was planning.

I mostly survived dinner, keeping quiet and deflecting all probing questions with the irritable one-word responses of a defiant mid-pubescent tyrant. After the meal, we walked to Minnesota's theatrical pride and joy—the Guthrie Theater. Throughout my life my mom, a beautiful parental curator of the arts, had consistently dragged my older sister and me to plays, art museums, and concerts all over the city. While there were a number of misses in there—*Sherlock Holmes: The Musical* definitely made the what-the-heck-is-happening-on-that-stage list—the Guthrie never disappointed. Located on the Mississippi River, it is widely known for its annual terrifying rendition of Charles Dickens's *A Christmas Carol.* The palpable joy of the Christmas spirit, mixed with the aroma of coffee and chocolate, created the perfect backdrop for the theatrical masterpiece. I mean if you weren't suicidal, obviously.

As we took our seats and waited for the show to begin, my mind drifted back to the last time I had seen this beautiful stage. My gaze shifted to the balcony where I had sat five years earlier with my closest friends from high school all dressed up and giggling louder than was socially acceptable. The light of our optimistic futures shone bright in our playful banter and reckless laughter. I was staring so intently at our seats from that night it began to feel real, as if I were having my own encounter with the Ghost of Christmas Past and he was taking me back to the archives of my story. Where had that fun and carefree kid I used to be disappeared to? He would be mortified to see the pitiful loser I'd become.

I was startled back from my daydream as the lights dimmed. The false warmth of the memory left me even more empty than before. As the familiar scenes moved along, the magical experience had the opposite of its intended effect on my frozen heart. With each costume change, my body swelled with bitterness and self-loathing. I didn't want to see that, like Scrooge, I too had a choice to change the ending to my story and find a better purpose to my life. As the actors took their bows, I immediately headed for the aisle, pushing through the sea of fancy theater patrons in order to disappear into the night faster than anyone could say, "Bah, humbug." I did not want to spend another second reflecting on the past, the present, or the little future I had left.

Like Scrooge, we all have times we're forced to look back over our lives: New Year's, birthdays, marking "single" on a wedding RSVP. So maybe a physical ghost doesn't show up and guide the tour, but it seems life is designed with natural pauses to evaluate where we've been and where we are going. Yet when life doesn't pan out the way we expect and it seems none of our dreams will ever come true, each of those reflection checkpoints can feel like a cigarette burn to the forearm—a torturous pain followed by a lingering, pungent sting.

If we're not careful, a series of bad life events or wrong turns can latch onto our identities like an undetected parasite eating away at the full life we were created to experience.

What has happened to us becomes who we are.

I made a mistake . . .
becomes *I am the mistake.*

I shouldn't have done that . . .
becomes *I can't deal with the pain.*

I never should have existed . . .
becomes *I'm desperate to end it.*

You don't ever think you will consider suicide—until the day you wake up holding a blade against your wrist.

I don't know a lot about God. I think He is real—not because some churchy man brainwashed me, but because when I finally started listening to His suggestions for a better life, I began to feel more alive. He didn't instantly heal my depression, and I've experienced more hurt in the hands of Christians than I would ever wish on anyone. But when I block out all the noise and arguing of modern-day religion and look for signs of a loving God in the world around me, I start to think we're all in this together. I start to think I am part of something bigger than myself in sacred things like love and friendship and helping someone who can never repay me. I look at a waterfall or a starfish or a newborn baby and can't help but wonder if the awe of this insanely beautiful world was not an accidental explosion of space gas, but rather a masterfully designed, breathtaking world of mystery and adventure.

I get why most of my generation has walked away from faith. Religion appears to be a failed experiment, with well-intentioned but flawed humans creating cultures of hierarchy, comfort, and busyness rather than wonder, questioning, and empathy. A Church of loving people has the potential to be one of the greatest gifts on the planet, but God can also be found around a bonfire, in a beautiful melody, or on the smiling face of a stranger. I have felt closest to God not in a big, expensive sanctuary but in the wild and reckless adventure of chasing after His purpose for my life.

For a long time, I thought I was an accident and I never should have existed. But God says we're all here on purpose, for a purpose, and He knew me before I was even in the womb.[1] Before my first heartbeat, He already loved me. With everything I've been through, that's a God I can get on board with.

I, too, think we're here on purpose.

To love deeply and help people however we can.

To forgive and heal and overcome.

To quietly gaze up at the stars and lose ourselves in enchanting stories.

To use our talents to make the world a better place.

To show up and let people see us for who we are.

To explore and conquer what most terrifies us.

To learn how to love God and be recklessly alive.

Your story was never meant to end prematurely. I can't wait another second to tell you suicide is not the answer. I promise you there's another way to stop the piercing pain in your heart. I promise you can find reasons to live and heal the darkness inside you. How do I know? Because I was sitting in that smelly, self-deprecating pigsty of pain you're in right now. That butt print next to you in the mud is mine.

You can overcome anything in your path. You can finally start to see you were made on purpose for a purpose. Your comeback starts now. Take my hand, my friend. Let's fight through this together.

———

Back in my bedroom, I slammed the door. Then my eye caught the open computer. I had dangerously left the letter up for anyone to see. As I sat down to resume the heart-breaking task, I was drawn into the white glow of the screen like a helpless mosquito entranced by a mesmerizing bug light. I reread the words I had written before Scrooge's festively rude interruption:

> You are the greatest person I have ever met. My heart is crumbling thinking I will never see you again, that I will never hear your contagious laughter or listen to your hilarious outlook on life. I could write a novel of everything you have done for me. For every terrible day you turned around, for every moment you were my strength when I had nothing left. Through all of the chaos, it's been you by my side. I am so sorry I won't be able to make it to your wedding, to meet your kids, to prank you in the nursing home. Just know that none of this is your fault. If anything, you are the hero of my story. Keep making this world a better place like you do

every day. I don't know what else to say
to you other than I will always love you.

I stared at the last sentence again before repeatedly pressing the delete button like a child attacking the elevator down arrow. I will always love you? Was I costarring in a Whitney Houston movie? She would have thought that was hilarious.

Physically and emotionally spent from the long, hard day, I clicked off the computer monitor and collapsed into bed. Soon the daily mental, self-loathing reruns began playing for the bajillionth time as I tried to drift off to sleep: *If seventeen-year-old Sam could see you now, he would be humiliated by what your life has become. You will forever be ugly and alone. You were an accident. You never should have existed.*

Six days left of feeling like Scrooge.

Six days until I would mail the letters.

Six days until all the pain would finally fade away.

PART TWO

CHAPTER 2

YOU CAN OWN YOUR STORY

AGE 8

I LIKED THE SPACE beneath the couch. It was safe and warm. I loved the way the rough, navy-blue carpet felt against my little second-grade face. I imagined the blue, floral-print sofa to be the long-lost sister of the magic bed from the classic 1971 film *Bedknobs and Broomsticks*— just three taps on its wooden feet and I could be cruising through the night sky or 10,000 leagues under the sea. The undercouch provided the perfect amount of space for me and only me and served as my cloak of invincibility. There was always that awkward moment when someone would sit on the couch and the ceiling would collapse downward ever so slightly, but even then it wasn't so bad unless the occupant proved to be particularly gassy.

I discovered my hideout during one of my parents' ear-splitting, neighbor-peering-over-the-fence yelling matches. Worse than the nights of chaos were the days that followed: hours of the loudest silence imaginable. The windows would rattle with the tension of our little family. Rare were the moments of peace and compassion. Sure, there were happy moments, too, but deep pain tends to darken even the brightest of memories.

One summer my family rented a cabin on what we Minnesotans call the North Shore (think Jersey Shore with more antiquing, more albino Norwegians, and less binge drinking). To every car passing our overstuffed, wood-paneled van, we must have looked like the American dream. For that week, at least, I think we were. My dad didn't bring any alcohol on that trip. It was one of the few times I can ever remember leaving our fifth family member, Uncle Budweiser, at home. The week was filled with card games and lighthouse tours, 1,000-piece colonial puzzles and wilderness hikes, Sven & Ole's scrumptious pizza, and, of course, the bear that came to dinner. There is a gold-framed painting of that week in the hallways of my mind. The engraved plate below it reads: What my family could have been.

My story is not superuncommon and doesn't begin to compare to the horror other people have survived. Still, tucked away in its dusty pages are years of struggle while wishing for a loving, present father. A dad who coached my baseball team like he'd promised. A dad who remembered to change my clothes before dropping me off at school. A dad who didn't tell me I ran like a girl. A dad who didn't disappear into a 24-pack every night when I needed help with my homework. A dad who would teach me even one of the prerequisite skills I needed to fit in with my male peers.

Instead of getting to be the coach's son, I eventually gave up on all sports.

Instead of relying on him to care for me, I learned to make meals and do my own laundry while my mom worked two jobs.

Instead of anything involving running, I gravitated toward music, where I wasn't bullied for my lack of masculinity.

Instead of asking for homework help, I found any excuse not to go home.

Instead of fishing with neighborhood boys, I sat on top of the couch and played video games by myself.

When things were really bad, my mom would whisk me away on incredible adventures to see train museums, pirate-ship playgrounds, and Titanic-sized ships passing through the locks and dams. But sometimes we couldn't escape, so we each learned to hide in our own ways.

I spent many hours in my little hideout, but after a while I got smart. When I could feel a fight coming on, I would put a pillow, a blanket, a few toy trains, and a snack under there to keep me occupied (although I never did quite solve the bathroom dilemma).

One day, it became evident this fight was bigger than most. Instead of a shorter burst of anger that could be quickly extinguished, flames of rage erupted and engulfed our entire three-bedroom home. As the intense interaction swept down the stairs into the basement, I slid the smudgy glass patio door open and hurled myself out of the line of destruction. I threw my body over the chain-link fence and ran as fast as my little feet could take me. Gasping for breath, I sprinted through backyard after backyard as if I had just escaped Alcatraz and was heading for the Pacific.

My white-blond hair took flight in the blur of my getaway as the shouting grew fainter behind me. After dodging cars across a busy street, I finally reached a thick, wooded sanctuary of preserved suburban wildlife just out of view of the road or nosey dog walkers. Panting like a puppy, I hobbled off the dirt path and found a place to sit atop a sea of decomposing leaves. Then I wiped some combination of sweat and tears from my face and took in a long, heavenly breath of freedom and silence.

The soft symphony of birds and the crisp rustling of leaves proved to be the perfect antidote to calm my adrenaline-fueled state. I looked around, taking in my new safe haven.

Maybe I won't go back.

My teacher had read us the story of Tom Sawyer, so I understood running away to become a pirate was always a viable option. Then my excitement faded. I didn't pack my one true friend, George the monkey, and I couldn't leave him behind in the mess.

What I wouldn't give for a different life.

———

I have spent most of my time on this planet asking God, "Why?"

Why has my life been turbulent?

Why does He allow His kids to suffer?

Why couldn't I have had an easy, normal life?

After years of childhood struggle, my brain developed into a minefield ready to explode without warning. Even as an adult, ongoing symptoms of post-traumatic stress disorder can unexpectedly detonate when a customer screams, forcing me to sprint for the exit before a panic attack sets in. Or when I'm attacked by an upset child at work. Or when graphic violence pops up in a movie or television show. Men are supposed to be strong and impenetrable; however, my body is conditioned to run, escape, and break down.

For almost two decades, I never talked to anyone about hiding under couches or being questioned by detectives when my dad was a person of interest in a murder case. I thought the only way to escape my deeply entrenched shame was to pretend none of the worst events ever happened. I left every painful scene of my biography on the cutting-room floor and only released the highly edited version to the general public.

But aren't you tired of hiding, my friend? Tired of wondering if someone will ever love you for who you really are? Tired of feeling empty and numb because it's been so long since you allowed yourself to hope and dream? Tired of believing the lie that things will never get better?

On my long healing journey, I learned if you want to be recklessly alive, you have to freaking own your story. You have to let go of anyone who tries to shame you for what you've endured. You have to stop worrying so stinkin' much about what anybody else thinks and start being true to the person God created you to be. You have to let people in and talk to someone who can help heal the wounds you never allow anyone to see.

I still have tough days, but never again will I hide under the couch of my life. You see, the boy hiding and escaping into the woods will always be a part of me. That brave, Thomas the Tank Engine–obsessed kid is the beginning of my redemption story, and his scenes deserve to be shared, not hidden. He has been hiding long enough.

After hours in the woods, the approaching darkness jolted me back to reality. The sun had mostly set, and being alone would soon terrify me. I hightailed it home even faster than my original escape, imagining fire trucks waiting outside my house and squad cars racing throughout the neighborhood to find me.

As I dashed toward the steps to the back door, I froze and let out a deep sigh of relief and disappointment. No one had noticed I was gone, and the yelling continued. I sat on the back steps and swatted at the summer gnats. Gazing at the galaxies above, I was strangely at ease. A peace within me surpassed all understanding.[2]

I heard the slam of the front screen door, the aggressive start of a car, and the fast, angry getaway from the driveway. All was safe for now. Waiting to make sure the coast was clear, I slid back in the house and grabbed my stuffed monkey from under the couch. I gently petted his head and hugged him close as I took in the disheveled life around me. I pressed my eyes closed and tried to re-create the peace of the woods.

Somehow, little George, we will get through this and everything will be alright.

CHAPTER 3

YOU CAN GET THE HELP YOU DESERVE

AGE 12

THE HONEY-OAK BAY WINDOW in the front of my childhood home was a canine's paradise with its beaming sunshine and unparalleled view of the neighborhood for optimal people watching. Okay, so we never had pets due to allergies, and, no matter what my mom says, fish do not count. Still, like our nonexistent black lab, at age twelve I, too, found great joy in climbing into the spacious, half-hexagon-shaped area of living room nirvana. This particular evening, though, the window was not a place of joy, but of anxiety and foreboding.

Storms had been brewing above my house since birth, but it had become obvious an F5 tornado was approaching, and it might be time to tie down the cows. I watched snakes of rain squirm across the large panes of glass. Then

I scanned up and down our long, hilly street and waited for any sign of headlights. *Dad should have been home from work hours ago.* I frenetically hit redial on our cordless phone for the sixteenth time. Every unanswered ring created an even tighter knot in my stomach. I paused for a millisecond before ringing his receptionist whom I wasn't supposed to call. Still no sign of life.

It's raining so hard. He must have been in an accident. Why hasn't he called?

Every detail of that night remains pristinely curated in my mind as if captured by a realist painter and hung with a sensor to keep it protected from the passage of time and from life's destructive oils. It was the autumn of my seventh-grade year and I, for once, had pulled straight As. My dad had always been one to impose the "get better grades than I got" parenting philosophy that, when coupled with my mom's natural teaching spirit, led me to some academic success. Report card in hand, I sat in the dogless window as hour after hour ticked by on my grandpa's clock that scowled at me from the varnished oak mantle.

As a result of our volatile homestead, I had become an unobtrusive child prone to excessive worrying that often manifested itself in the relentless chewing of every T-shirt neck I owned. The recklessness of my father created in me a boy who played it safe and never rocked the boat, thank you very much. I became a peacemaker, a gentle soul, a decorated sergeant of kindness and equality. When playing board games by myself, I often let the imaginary opponents win—because obviously sometimes they deserved to be victorious, too.

Somewhere around the time Mark McGwire and Sammy Sosa were chasing home run records, my dad started sleeping on the couch I liked to hide under. One scorching and lazy midsummer's evening, I drifted off to dreamland with my dad beside me in our overstuffed green leather chair as the laughing track of *I Love Lucy* reruns droned on. I awoke during the night's scariest hour, shivering alone in our family room with the lights off. As I dragged my feet up the stairs, the hairs on the back of my neck leapt to attention. Someone was in my bed. My Thomas the Tank Engine comforter was covering a six-foot-four-inch musty, drunken Goldilocks. I sighed. *Well, I guess my dad deserves a good night of sleep, too.* I grabbed a blanket from the wooden toy chest, fluffed the neon-green eighties carpet, and resolved to spend my night on the floor. *See, it's not so bad.*

A few hours later I awoke to the sounds of sizzling bacon and hangover gagging coming from the kitchen. Just another morning in utopia.

Even in his most selfish moments, I never hated my dad. In fact, there are parts of his spirit that still dance among my greatest passions. An avid writer and aspiring sports author, Art (his most popular alias) helped me get my first article published in the city newspaper. Not to mention he was a buzz-fueled jokester who served as an attentive audience for the honing of my early stand-up comedy routines.

Perhaps the greatest gift he gave my sister and me was a regular ride to Sunday school. That is, if we got ourselves ready and woke him up. Our Eaton nuclear family of four embodied an exclusive Christmas and Easter tradition, and, though we had a reputation of snoring in the corner pew, we never missed these two high Episcopalian holidays. While Art avoided church with the wildness of a rebellious teenager, I slowly fell in love with the quaint and safe building and its faded parking-lot basketball hoop. That place felt different than the chaos which seemed to permeate my life outside its compassionate brick walls.

Despite his more positive qualities, there isn't much about my dad I admired as a man or father. His inability to hold a job or provide any sort of stable income plagued much of our lives. My mom, the hardest-working woman I have ever known, kept our family afloat through every car repossession and home foreclosure with her job in the bakery at our local grocery store. Despite her struggles at home, she greeted morning customers with the warmest of smiles as she handed them a piece of freshly baked Danish ecstasy. She was a beautiful soul ensnared in the nets of abuse and disillusionment. In a different generation that frowned upon divorce in any circumstance, her mother had taught her, "Your husband is your life." My mom exuded the strength that held us together in the worst of times and is the reason we made it out alive.

As I stared down at my now-crinkled report card, my arm tingled with the imaginary heart attack of reality. He wasn't coming home. The man in the moon sneered down at me from behind the disheartened clouds, judging the boy awake hours past his school-night bedtime. I balled up the report card and tossed it on the floor before locking the front door. As the click of the lock set into place, so did the deadbolt at the entrance to my heart.

———

Somewhere in the house that is my mind, there is a room—a room which no one is allowed to see. It lies behind an inconspicuous door that goes undetected on the walking tour. Behind its lock and three deadbolts lies a dark and empty space, no furniture or decoration to be seen. The dull hardwood floors are dirty and worn from years of pacing feet and neglected housekeeping. The sole window is boarded up and sealed to perfection in order to block out even a single rogue ray of light that may attempt to shine a sliver of hope into the clandestine space. The stale smell of mothballs hangs in the air, intermingling with the penetrating odor of disappointment and heartbreak.

The walls are the color of a restless night and appear smooth to the naked eye. Upon further investigation, raised words can be seen upon their surface like a wallpaper of scars. When I step back, a lifetime of painful stories reveals itself on every inch from floor to ceiling. As my hand traces each letter for the millionth time, the words cut through as if someone were carving them deep into my skin. This room is a place I have spent too many hours of my life. It is a room called depression.

I first discovered this space shortly after the night of the report card. I didn't know what I was creating when I walked in. I just knew I wanted to be alone—completely alone. This room gave me the illusion of safety by keeping everyone at arm's length. Never trust, never be real, never allow anyone in so you won't self-destruct when they abandon you. It wasn't until years later—the months I spent planning to take my own life—I realized I couldn't escape. I was living my own Hotel California; I could check out anytime I liked, but I could never leave. Despite the mirage of safety, when I'm there, this torturous chamber encapsulates the complete absence of love.

I still get lured into this terrible room sometimes even now, with its voice that taunts: You are ugly and worthless. You will always be a loser. No one will ever love you.

I'm sorry your mind can be a scary place.

I'm sorry your brain loops the trauma.

I'm sorry that sleep can be the only relief.

I'm sorry the pills didn't help at first.

I'm sorry you feel completely alone.

I'm sorry a good day can be just staying alive.

I'm sorry ignorant dirtbags call you weak.

I'm sorry you're told to "be more positive."

I'm sorry people have abandoned you.

I'm sorry you stay in when you can't fake it.

I'm sorry for all of it.

I wish I could wave a magic wand and heal you, but, much to my chagrin, I am not an all-powerful supergod of the universe. (I was shocked, too.) There is, however, more help available than ever before. There is better research and an army of us dropkicking the crap out of the stigma. There are opportunities to participate in talk therapy, support groups, and online communities. There are more mental health coaches and better-informed doctors. There is a world full of people waiting to help you, but you have to ask—and keep asking.

Please don't spend another second locked in your stupid dark room. Life won't always be this unbearable.

If you want to be recklessly alive, stop suffering in silence. You don't have to fight this alone. You can ask for the help you deserve.

As I brushed my teeth in our green-tiled bathroom, the rain finally stopped falling. I wiped the tears from my eyes and accepted what I had to do. I didn't want my dad to leave, but we all knew where he was and who he was spending the night with. I had immense hopes for him to turn his life around, to quit drinking and be present, to finally kick Uncle Budweiser to the curb and help us become the beautiful family we were meant to be. But the time had come to accept that fantasy would never be a reality. It was time to grow up and stop pretending he would ever change. It was time to move on to the next chapter of our lives.

When I got home from school the next day, I would sit down with my mom and sister and talk about what we knew but weren't saying. My mom deserved better. We all did.

I picked up the balled-up report card and tossed it in the trash. I flicked off the bedroom lights and tried to silence the disappointment exploding in my chest. I had no idea what would happen next, but I had to believe whatever lay ahead would be better than the life we were leaving behind. I mean, regardless of how this whole family disaster turned out, I did have freaking straight As.

CHAPTER 4

YOU CAN FIGHT BACK

AGE 13

MY EYES EXPLODED OPEN. Someone was trying to break into our already broken home. An apocalyptic crash echoed up the green-wallpapered hallway as our puny brass lock held on for dear life. In an instant, the world went quiet. I attempted to convince myself I had imagined the commotion—just like the Nobel Prize–winning blonde does in every horror movie right before she gets whacked.

A second later another thump bellowed even louder, as the intruder upped his force. Launching to my feet like a trained ninja, I reached for the engraved Chicago Cubs bat on the floor next to my bed. My hands shook as reality registered through my groggy state. The oak slugger lay polished and unused, but perhaps this night would be its rookie debut.

After the long report-card night, my sister, my mom, and I sat down to talk about the mess we were living in. A few days later I came home to see my dad sobbing at the kitchen table with our white, cordless landline pressed to his ear. My mom gave him the ultimatum: he had to choose once and for all between his affair and his family.

I peeked around the corner of our dated 1970s chocolate-brown kitchen and heard my grandma's soft, concerned voice escape out of the phone receiver. Dad looked at me with red, drunken eyes. The finality of the night's events seemed to be sobering him up against his will. Complacent to our life of pandemonium and extreme emotions, I didn't even recognize this was the night of no return. As I continued to watch the dramatic scene play out, I saw a side of my mom that had been dormant for far too many years. Her backbone was tall and fierce. Momma grizzly was out to fight. She was done being pushed around and abused, she was done letting this man consume and embezzle her hard-earned money, she was done being cheated on and taken for granted. I looked at this guy with whom I shared DNA and saw a hollow shell of a life wrecked by alcohol addiction. My insides wrenched with compassion for him and all that he was losing by walking away.

I tiptoed up to my bedroom, slammed the door, and took stock of the wreckage of clothes and toys that littered every inch of my eight-by-eight-foot room. (Please, I attended gifted classes, and everyone knows real geniuses are messy.) For reasons unknown to me at the time, I started cleaning.

I slowly picked up the game pieces scattered on the floor next to a pile of dirty basketball uniforms. I returned all of the stuffed animals to my Thomas the Tank Engine bedspread and threw away the remaining garbage on the floor. After my unexpected cleaning spree, I climbed on top of my comforter and looked around at the newfound order within as the chaos ruminated beyond my door.

Sometime later, that door opened to my mom's warm smile. Her optimistic eyes had returned like a long-lost friend. She bent down, kissed me on the head, and pulled the comforter over my middle-school body like I was back in nursery school.

"Tomorrow things will be better," she whispered. Then she pushed down the train light switch and closed the door. I was alone in the darkness again.

"Let me see my kids! They are *my* kids!" The insane, intoxicated voice carried throughout the neighborhood. The burglar's voice sent more fear than a complete stranger's: it was my estranged father.

The neighbor's kitchen light flipped on. Dogs barked in the distance. Wrigley bat in hand, I crept to my bedroom door and opened it a sliver. All kids want their dad to be Superman, to defeat the bad guy and come to their aid, but that would never be my papa. On this night my dad was the misunderstood nemesis. He was Lex Luthor.

I can't fully explain to you what it's like to be terrified of your own DNA. To have to decide at age thirteen whether to give your dad endless chances or put three new dead bolts on the front door. To feel the heavy burden of being the only man left to turn your family tree around.

We develop so many of our self-beliefs early in life, but when exactly do the lies take root in our minds? Was it the tenth time my dad didn't come to my baseball game, or was it the night of the report card? Was it the year the girl in English class asked me loudly every day if I was gay yet, or all the days the guy on the bus punched me and called me assface? Was it the aunt who said at Christmas, "Wow, Sam's getting fat," or was it the first time I searched "the most painless way to kill yourself"?

Some people who have been hurt spend their whole lives trying to hurt the world back. And some of us bury that pain deep within.

We sabotage relationships before the other person can leave us.

We lose touch with friends because we can't tell them we're barely hanging on.

We don't trust a God who would give us a story filled with hurt and despair.

We never chase our wildest dreams because we're always waiting for someone to break down the front door and drag us back into a past nightmare.

But that's no way to live, my friend. In fact, that's not living at all. You weren't created to spend your nights beating yourself up and cowering in fear. If you want to be recklessly alive, you have to get out of bed and fight back. Pick up the metaphorical bat and say, *"Enough!* I will not spend the next thirty years hating myself. I will not let trauma rob another second of the precious days I have left. I will not be silenced about my pain ever again. I will not sit here and let anyone stop me from taking my life back."

You have the power to get help, escape the abuse, and change your life. You are strong enough to overcome anyone trying to hold you down. You can pick yourself up and dust off the past. You can pick up your baseball bat and fight back.

In the silhouette of the night, my mom's voice grew sharp. She began talking down the drunk as she had done for most of their marriage. After a few more conversational bouts, my mom managed to force the door shut again. The broken security chain dangled against the door. I heard the slamming of Dad's Jeep door and the sound of flying gravel beneath his worn-out tires. His villainous words hung in the cold night air: "You can't keep my kids from me."

My mom came back up the stairs. Through my half-open bedroom door, I could see tears streaming down her beautiful face in the yellow haze of the hallway light. Still shaking from the adrenaline, I stood silently in the darkness of my room. Her eyes met mine as she gave me a smile that said we will get through this. Together we were learning that sometimes the safest way out of the storm is to roll the windows up and drive straight into the worst of it. Sometimes, the only way out is through.

She flipped the switch on the hallway light, and darkness returned. The cheetah of my heartbeat finally slowed back to a casual prowl. I pulled the covers up over my head. With the cold sweat of fear dripping from my forehead, I grasped my one-eyed and well-loved Curious George stuffed animal against my stomach and began to sob.

An emotional mess after hours of tossing and turning, I walked into my mom's room. "I can't sleep in my room. I think there are mice."

Climbing into her queen-sized bed, I still clutched the bat beneath the covers. I prayed for him to try to come back and try to break in again. No one was going to hurt me or my family. I wasn't going to be afraid of this man for one more day.

CHAPTER 5

YOU CAN MAKE IT THROUGH THE SH*T

AGE 16

I PUNCHED MY CARD in the old time clock and pushed my way through the swinging employees' door. Now entering my junior year of high school, I hadn't seen my dad in two years, and I was better for it. I brushed aside my shaggy bangs and walked onto the store floor like I owned the place. Looking at the daily jobs clipboard, I discovered my name was crossed out under *bagger* and instead was scribbled next to the column titled *maintenance* (their politically correct term for storewide indentured cleaning servant). Rather than laughing with my favorite Sunday-morning customers, I would be pushing around an odorous garbage can, mopping the accident-prone pickle-jar aisle, and cleaning the bathrooms every hour on the hour because, despite humanity's many modern advances, full-grown adults still struggle to comprehend that the floor isn't where one should place his used toilet paper.

As I worked through my checklist—cleaning streaky mirrors, emptying half-filled garbage cans so they never appeared full, and wiping up the morning doughnut crumbs from the breakroom—I was paged through the storewide speakers.

"Sam Eaton, dial 416. Sam Eaton, 4-1-6. Thank you."

A personal page was never a good sign in this dirty line of work.

"The toilets are overflowing. Close them immediately and report back."

I scrambled across the large suburban food oasis toward the customer restrooms I'd left in pristine condition only thirty minutes prior. Rounding the corner, a small trail of water creeped out under the men's door, and I knew I was in deep shit. I clasped the plunger and raced to the raging porcelain throne. The store manager slammed the door open and released a not-so-professional expletive as the wealthy, unfazed patrons nearby continued sipping extra-large frou-frou coffee beverages.

As I plunged with all my might, the bowl's contents repeatedly overflowed the sides, covering the floor with enough water for a toddler kiddie pool. Finally, with one last heroic pump, the sweetest gulping sound emerged, and water slowly retreated down the drain. I wiped the sweat—at least I hoped it was sweat—from my forehead and looked around at the hours of cleaning ahead of me. Believing the worst was over, I was jolted when the manager exclaimed, "It's coming up by the salad bar now!"

Of course it is.

Wading through water up to my ankles, I looked out to see a steady stream of bathroom waste emerging from the drain between the salad bar and mostly empty restaurant seating.

"I have an emergency plumber on the way, but he can't be here for at least an hour."

I grabbed the wet vac from the closet, unscrewed the metal drain cover, and began vacuuming up the liquid and partially solid waste from the surrounding area. Racing to empty the vacuum into the mop closet, back and forth I went in an endless cycle of minimum-wage hell. As I placed cones and caution tape on both ends of the walkway, the epic battle between teenager and human waste waged on.

An hour into the disaster, an entitled customer ripped my caution tape in order to make his own gourmet salad. With one hand still on the vacuum hose, I kindly said, "My apologies, sir. This area is temporarily closed due to a pipe issue." He tersely replied, "I'm just getting my salad," rolled his eyes, and pushed his cart through puddles of sewage. Several minutes later, another woman again took down the caution tape. Dressed for the opera, she moved toward the salad bar and glared at me—as if not getting her salad were the equivalent of my murdering the toy poodle popping out of her purse. Her much younger man friend followed behind, pointed to a brown chunk, and asked nonchalantly, "Is that a turd?"

Glancing down at my watch, I realized I was now two hours into fighting this losing battle, with still no sign of this so-called plumber messiah. I was also ninety minutes past my break, but it goes without saying, I wasn't interested in eating—perhaps ever again.

Kids, if you're reading this, let this one poopy story of my life at sixteen prove that high school probably isn't going to be the best four years of your life.

Yes, there were many wonderful moments. I had the greatest group of friends any guy could ask for. I got to make incredible music with the best choir teachers on the planet. I was blessed to spend beautiful weekends at cabins and the beach, laughing until my sides hurt. But there were moments of such intense bullying, I sobbed for an hour after school. There were moments I hated how hard my mom, sister, and I had to work just to make ends meet, while so many of my peers donned $150 pre-ripped Abercrombie jeans and complained about how expensive parking passes were from their shiny, red convertibles. There were moments when I wasn't sure I wanted to be alive.

In class, I went from never missing the honor roll to barely getting Bs and Cs. Unable to focus, I often lost myself in sad daydreams and wanted to disappear. Hiding within baggy, hooded sweatshirts, I doodled in every notebook:

efily metah i
efily metah i
efily metah i
efily metah i

My backward code of *I hate my life*.

When I think of the most painful moments of my existence, I like to picture this crazy-compassionate and recklessly loving God sitting next to me. For a long time, I couldn't reconcile His love for me with a world over-flowing with violence and hate. Yet, as I spent more time getting to know the Big Guy, I started to believe He gives us all complete control of how we choose to live our lives. Unfortunately, some people use their free will to be complete scumbags.

There have been several seasons I had to bite down hard and suffer through it. Times when I had to put my nose down and take life one hour at a time. Times when getting through the next bus ride, the next unit test, or the next eight-hour shift seemed unbearable.

When you're up to your neck in it, you can't always see how the toilet of your life will ever stop overflowing. But it does. Maybe not today or the next day, but when you ask for help, work hard, and trudge through the best you can, I promise you can make it to the other side.

Whatever you're going through, you can survive the worst life has to throw at you. You can put your nose down and work hard until it's over. You can make it through the sh*t.

Three and a half hours after the call was placed, the plumber finally rounded the corner. I looked at him with hallowed eyes, as if I'd just finished twenty-four hours working in the emergency room in Spain during the Running of the Bulls. He laughed at my disheveled appearance. I turned off the vacuum without saying a word. Within minutes he had shut off the water. Shell-shocked and changed, I slowly exited the battlefield.

Walking to the front of the store, my manager handed me two movie tickets as a thank-you for seeing a crap job through to the bitter end.

"Would you like to go home early?"

I looked at the other baggers in their pressed uniforms. They smiled and joked with each other during an unusually slow Sunday, and I imagined how different this day could have been.

The manager chuckled. "Someday we will joke about this, Sam." Without any inkling of a response, I plodded toward my rusty Plymouth Breeze. Rolling down the windows, I attempted to alleviate the stench of my battle. As I threw myself into the shower still clothed, the water at my feet ran brown. Taking off my uniform, I scrubbed every inch of my lanky teenage body until my skin was red like a sunburn, unable to clear the smell from my nose even after twenty minutes and half a bottle of body wash.

After toweling off, I rubbed my hand over my wet hair. Feeling the urge to alleviate my bladder, I approached the toilet and froze.

On second thought, I'll hold it.

CHAPTER 6

YOU CAN FIGHT THE LIES IN YOUR BRAIN

AGE 20

"ARE YOU STUPID?" HE said, staring at me over the rims of his pretentious eyeglasses. "Are you really that stupid?"

I didn't speak. I was using every ounce of my strength to not let a single tear emerge from my eyes, because that's what this man—my college voice professor—lived for.

"You can't even respond when I'm asking you a question?"

His authoritative voice rang at the decibel level of an AC/DC concert for hours after each of my weekly voice lessons and confirmed my greatest struggles: *I'm not good at anything. I'm stupid and worthless. I never should have chased this dream.*

Springtime had arrived early in our sleepy college town, but I was so stressed out with my course load I hadn't noticed. Incessant handholding permeated every common area as the "ring by spring" ladies either anxiously awaited the big proposal (thus signifying ultimate victory) or, more commonly, made one final marital push by shortening their skirts to a length that matched their level of husband desperation. The instant I'd stepped out of the car on my first day at Luther College, the warm and sacred soil felt like home. Tucked away in the picturesque bluffs of northeast Iowa, Luther has the greatest undergraduate choral program on the planet. What better place to become a choir director?

Many of the adults in my atmosphere never quite knew what to say when I told them I was majoring in music. The close-minded ones made colorful jokes about how my older sister was fighting terrorism in Afghanistan while I decided to hold hands with hippies, sing Kumbaya, and dance naked around a bonfire. After arriving on campus, I realized their ideas weren't that far off from some of my more free-spirited classmates, but, much to their surprise, that was never quite my scene. However, to be safe, let's keep the games of naked soccer between you and me.

"Sixty percent of music majors drop out or switch majors before their third year," my professor said on the first day of freshman music theory. Not quite the welcome-to-college speech I had expected. My imagination morphed him into Professor Snape from Harry Potter telling me to turn to page 394. As I glanced around at my classmates, I believed I would make it. I had what it took to be a music teacher who inspired and changed lives the way so many of my teachers had done for me. I could persevere to graduation, and no one could stop me.

"Sit," he said sharply. "It's not too late to change your major."

I stared deep into his eyes, as joy slid off my face and shattered on the floor. I was three semesters away from becoming the first person in my family to get a four-year degree. Why in the name of student debt would I consider changing my major now? For three years I worked three jobs, juggled nineteen credits each semester, studied piano and voice lessons, sang in the Nordic Choir, barely slept—and now he thought I should quit?

"I don't think you have what it takes."

Perhaps I should have found a new teacher right then and there. I tried to talk to the department head about my terrible experiences, but I was met with the less-than-helpful advice to "tough it out." So, for sixty minutes every week, I kept grinding through toward graduation with this emotionally abusive and pompous human. To be perfectly fair, I did learn a few things from him. Most prominently, the type of teacher I never wanted to be.

At the end of the school year, we were five months away from my required senior recital—thirty minutes of memorized, center-stage singing in a world-class recital hall full of people half smiling and fully judging. Three years of hard work toward this pressure-filled, stomach-cramping experience, and now it was just around the riverbend. At my final lesson before summer break, we started rehearsing the twelve-page aria he had picked to close my program. When I made a rhythmic mistake, he slammed the lid down on the piano and stared out the window like he might burst into some sort of murderous aria himself. A brutally awkward amount of silence passed until he turned to face me.

"I don't want my name on your recital program. I think it's best if you find another teacher."

My vision blurred as the world gave out beneath my feet. Years of trying to please this barbaric professor, and he was dropping me? Years of working on everything he said, beating myself up over my mistakes and "lack of talent." Years of walking out of his office in tears, desperate to be good at the one thing I loved the most. After all of that, his message was this: You are detestable. Your existence embarrasses me. Get out of my life.

And there I was again, abandoned by another man in my greatest hour of need and pondering suicide.

I moved home for the summer boiling with rage and swollen from the shock of his hateful words. However, I did what you have to do in the hardest times. After a few weeks, I forced myself out of bed and determined to find any way possible to make the recital happen.

I reached out to my high school voice teacher, who came to my rescue. She was one of the people who had taught me to be proud of who I am, to stand tall, and to sing with the passion that burned deep within me. Our lessons were filled with roaring laughter and silly faces. She started to pick up the splintered pieces of my confidence as we planned my recital. "You can do this, Sammy Eaton," she said and grinned from behind the piano.

I returned for my final semester and was assigned a new voice teacher. As I walked into her office, she swiveled in her chair and said, "I've heard some things about you." (Evidently, the old voice teacher had told everyone in the department I was impossible to work with and, to save face, denied ever telling me to find a new teacher.) "Tell me the truth. Are you only switching to me because you've heard I am a pushover?" When she said this, tears overtook the tall dam of my struggling eyes. I told her what I had been through, and she wept, too. Although she had known me for only a few minutes, she wrapped me in an enormous bear hug that felt as if I'd known her my entire life. She grabbed the sides of my head in her palms, looked deep into my reddened eyes, and said exactly what I needed to hear.

"I am so sorry for what you have been through. We're going to get you through this recital." And off we went.

My guess is we all have experienced a voice that tells us we are never good enough. My other professors were beautiful humans who loved me and invited me to their homes for dinner. One of my conducting professors told me his only regret seeing me graduate was that his kids were too old to have me as their teacher. My piano teacher told me after one of my performances that she had never heard that heartbreaking piece performed better by a student in her entire thirty-year teaching career. Yet I'm sure you can guess which voice I allowed to dominate my thought life and shape my worth.

In his voice studio, he was my god. I elevated his opinion higher than Marilyn Monroe's skirt while walking over an air vent. I gave him the power to obliterate me because I didn't realize I had a choice. I accepted his words as truth because, as he made clear, I could have an opinion when I earned my doctorate degree. He was living proof of every horrible thing I believed about myself through the years of hiding under the couch and cowering with a baseball bat in hand. His voice matched that of the bullies who whispered, *The world would be better off without you.*

I know your mind can be a scary place when agonizing words and painful memories loop out of control until you're a sobbing mess. I'm sorry a few hateful people hijacked your confidence and self-worth. I'm sorry your brain has been conditioned to self-destruct. But how many more years are you going to spend hating yourself? How many more years are you going to suffer without giving healing everything you've got?

You don't have to be a victim to your own mind. You are strong enough to fight back. Identify the voices in your head and where they came from. Intercept the accusing words with truth and empathy. Replace those thoughts with a voice that sounds like someone supporting you and celebrating your progress.

While I imagine I will always have universe-sized questions about God, learning to hear His voice was a game-changer for me.

Depression says no one truly loves you, but God says He has loved you since before you were in the womb.[3]

Depression says you are worthless, but God says you are loved with an everlasting love.[4]

Depression says you are ugly and disgusting, but God says you are made in His image[5]; outside appearances don't matter.[6]

Depression says you are completely alone, but God says He will never leave you or forsake you.[7]

Depression says you have made too many mistakes, but God says you are a new creation.[8]

Depression says you are stupid, but God says you are fearfully and wonderfully made.[9]

Depression says your situation is impossible, but God says with Him all things are possible.[10]

Depression says to stay in the stupid dark room where no one can hurt you, but Jesus says He is the light of the world[11]; He came so we may have life and have it to the fullest.[12]

You can't be recklessly alive if you are your own worst enemy. You don't have to give into the voices in your head that scream you are stupid. You can and you will learn to fight the lies in your brain.

The morning of my senior recital, I opened my student mailbox to find a note from my pathetic voice teacher: "I regret to inform you I will be out of town for your recital. Break a leg." I contemplated responding on the back, "I regret to inform you that you are an asshole," but instead, I ripped it up, threw it in the recycle bin, and moved on with my life.

At 7:00 p.m. on November 5, I proudly walked onto the mahogany stage of the Jenson-Noble Hall of Music. Intense performance lights blinded my view of most of the audience as I worked my way through song cycles in English, French, and German.

With only one song remaining, I locked eyes with my best friend and recital partner, Jen. She gave me a quick hand squeeze before the introduction to our final duet. The audience roared with laughter as we sang "The Song That Goes Like This" from the musical *Spamalot*—our passive-aggressive jab at the closed-minded classical voice department that had largely turned its back on both of us.

As the song ended, a wave of relief moved throughout my entire body like a cool breeze off the lake. Our super-fans jumped to their feet in celebration of all that we had accomplished. I looked out into the audience, caught the eye of Professor Williams, my life-saving voice teacher, and mouthed, "Thank you." She nodded a gentle acknowledgment while lifting her applauding hands toward the stage. A deep smile floated from her face into my healing heart.

Jen and I took our final bows and held our heads high as we exited backstage. We hugged each other as tightly as two people possibly can in a suit and classy ball gown. We leapt as we shouted, "We did it!" And then we downed many beers in the name of blood, sweat, and arias.

CHAPTER 7

YOU CAN FORGIVE YOURSELF

AGE 22

IN A DREAMY, SMALL-TOWN coffee shop that made every basic, big-city tourist shout, "Oh, for cute," while secretly yearning for the monotony of a Starbucks, her fingers reached across the well-worn mahogany table to comfort mine. I harshly pulled my hand back. Despite the love between us that even non-English-speaking eavesdroppers could detect without subtitles, hurtful words continued to pour out of my mouth like self-sabotaging, can't-get-close-to-anyone, antirelationship word vomit.

If you zoomed out on all of my love stories, you'd see essentially the same sitcom rerun with different haircuts and similar outcomes. (At one point, it was rumored the government was considering putting out a health warning against dating me, but luckily, due to their inability to complete anything, the law died on the House floor.)

This beautiful woman, however, was the type of person I'd always imagined marrying, and I had thrown everything into making her fall in love with me.

The doorbell rang on my ragtag second floor of a gross old house. I glanced at my surroundings and smiled. When I had the capacity, I was an incredible boyfriend. I moved toward the 8x8 living room that donned my questionable thrift-store green plaid couch and saw heaven in the smile of this girl, perched on her tiptoes, peeking through the glass front door. For one brief moment, the entire universe felt like everything was working out how it was meant to. When I opened the door, she handed me a gift bag and a pan of brownies. We hugged for so long that, out in the wild, anti-PDA extremists would have thrown garbage at us. Our hips swayed slightly as if we were about to slow dance, and that rare feeling of knowing you're not alone in the world eclipsed all the fear I had about opening my heart to the girl with the Wisconsin necklace.

We moved toward the horrendously designed hallway-turned-miniature-kitchen, and Christmas-morning-like excitement fluttered in my stomach.

"So, what is this 'life-changing' meal you're cooking for me?" she exclaimed with air quotes, jousting with the first bout of our usual flirtatious banter.

"Not so fast, brownie queen. First, open that door."

"The spare bedroom? Why?"

She looked at me and hesitated—probably wondering if I had hired a murderous-looking clown to scare her. Then she opened the door. String lights crisscrossed a room containing camping chairs, a portable television, a light-up paper campfire, and two bedsheets draped over a rope above a blow-up mattress. She glanced back quizzically.

"You said you'd never been camping, so I thought we'd do a practice run since it's February."

She dove into my arms, wrapped her hands around my waist, and pressed her face into my tall and lanky chest. She squeezed tight, and I kissed the top of her head. *This might be it.* My hopeless romantic, twenty-two-year-old brain showing itself in spades. As we sat on a blanket on the kitchen floor, Ingrid Michaelson quietly serenaded our candlelit dinner, while the sound of hot dogs sizzling in a pan echoed like grease-fueled applause. Afterwards, with the windows fogged and lights low, we danced and laughed with the chemistry romantic comedy directors can only pray their leading couple can fake. Here we were, living the broke-indie, college love story millennial dream. She grabbed my hand. I squeezed tightly to say without words that we had made it through the hardest part of our relationship and could finally just be happy.

She smiled. "Tell me about your biggest dreams," she said, always moving our conversations into deeper territory.

As the night moved along, we cozied up in the makeshift tent. It kept falling down on us, but hey, most guys are so lame anyone with an ounce of romantic creativity seems somewhere in the league of Ryan Gosling. She was tucked under my arm, with her ear pressed against the indent of my chest.

The perfect girl. The perfect night.

Sadly, when you've lived a life littered with trauma, waiting for the other shoe to drop is second nature. Fear began attacking my heart. As Charlie Brown famously said, "I think I'm afraid to be happy because whenever you get too happy, something bad always happens." Preach, Charlie Brown. Preach.

I closed my eyes and tried to brush aside the anxiety. An hour later, I woke to her kissing me, her warm breath tickling my upper lip while the credits rolled on yet another movie I'd slept through.

"Stay asleep. I'll see you tomorrow."

Despite wanting to drift back to my dreams, I opened my eyes to take a long gaze at this beautiful girl I got to call mine. Still half-awake, I thought in my head the word I had never said to anyone. Then my eyes flew wide open.

Holy Crap. Did I just think the L-word?

She squinted and turned her head to the side, always trying to guess what was happening in my mind. I jumped to my feet to walk her out. One more long kiss at the door and she was gone, back down the rickety wooden steps into the night. I looked around at the camping decor throughout my apartment, rubbed my eyes, and smiled.

She's the one.

A few weeks later, we sat in our corner booth with our now room-temperature coffee, trying to hang on to the love we'd spent the better part of eighteen months cultivating. On the wall beside us, a "Livin' La Vida Mocha" sign mocked our misery.

In the middle of my first year of teaching high school in small-town Iowa, the demons that were quieted by the excitement of graduating college and landing my first job returned in the dead of winter. She was the one good thing in my life and everything I ever wanted. Unfortunately, I was a complete mess of a human being. I had never been to counseling. I had never come to terms with my dad leaving. I had never once sought help for my suicidal thoughts. I was living in a small town with almost no friends my age. Despite loving her more than any person I had previously met, something uncontrollable within me was screaming to leave her before she left me.

Surely, I would ruin her life. I would never be good enough for her. Her parents would hate me for my student-loan debt. She deserved a better man. Somebody else could make her happier. I would end up a burden she would ultimately resent. I would never be the strong Christian man she deserved. If she ever saw the darkness within me, she would run screaming from my life. I had to save her from myself.

———

This scene has haunted me more than any other—even more than the sexual abuse I experienced as a kid. I've replayed it in my mind a million times, unable to forgive myself for the choice I made. If I'm honest, I'm not sure I'll ever fully get over losing someone I loved so deeply. The regret wasn't instant. It was a long, slow awakening that seeped up to the surface months later. That deep hole that led to the breakup was a version of myself I didn't even recognize. As soon as I started to feel better, I began to experience the gut-wrenching pain of the hurt I had caused and what I had lost.

The only way I can even begin to forgive myself is to accept that this disease called depression, which distorts reality, stopped me from going after what I truly wanted. The night of the report card taught me to self-sabotage and lock myself in a stupid dark room where no one could hurt me. The deeply engrained voice screaming, "Are you stupid, are you really that stupid?" still hijacked my ability to see anything good within me. A healed, whole-hearted version of myself could have spent a lifetime loving her, but a broken, barely-hanging-on kid with garbage bags full of unresolved trauma did the best he could and failed.

It's taken me a really long time to forgive twenty-two-year-old Sam for that day. While forgiving others can feel so freaking hard, forgiving ourselves can be the greatest challenge of all. But there's a beautiful promise in the Bible that says, "As far as the east is from the west, so far has he removed our transgressions from us."[13] With the help of God and a cool therapist, I've been able to forgive myself and let that mistake disappear behind the horizon.

If you want to be recklessly alive, you have to do the hard work of inner healing so you can finally move on. It's time to forgive yourself. Hating yourself won't bring anyone back.

She reached for my hand. Once again, I pulled it away. Not wanting to see the depths of her heartbreak, I struggled to meet her eyes. We stared at each other in a silent stalemate. Each minute felt like a year.

"This can't be it," she choked out.

She repeated it again and again as I took a match to the photo album of our future together. The four beautiful kids. The playful black lab. The wrap-around porch on our country dream home.

"This can't be it," she said, almost inaudibly, one more time.

I looked up, taking in the most beautiful woman— inside and out—I had ever known. All I wanted was her and a red flannel blanket for the rest of my life, but all I could feel was an unstoppable pull toward the door.

"I'm sorry. I can't do this," I muttered.

Barely opening my mouth, I said the worst lie of my entire life: "I don't love you." Then I walked out into the cold Iowa night.

CHAPTER 8

YOU CAN CHOOSE A DIFFERENT PATH

AGE 23

AFTER FINISHING MY FIRST year of teaching in Iowa, I moved back home to Minnesota and quickly found myself in a lot of downtown bar-type establishments because, well, that's what every early twenty-something does, obviously. Far too many nights during that season were spent in the seductive city nightlife of strobe lights, ear-damaging N-TS, N-TS, N-TS music, and the alluring feeling of losing control after a few too many drinks.

Before leaving for college, I promised the universe I would never drink. I had seen first hand the death grip alcohol held on much of my family and swore with every ounce of my out-of-shape body I would never go near the stuff. By my sophomore year of college, however, I was well educated in Jäger bombs, beer pong, flippy cup, quarters, avoiding resident assistants, bathtub gin, and thirty-seven hangover cures (most of them involving the McDonald's drive-thru). I loved this new, wild way of life. I thought it helped me overcome the worst things I believed about myself: I was awkward, quiet, boring, straitlaced, and forgettable. Within an hour, I could become the life of the party and fully buy into the illusion that this liquor-infused affection meant I was finally liked.

After college, this lifestyle still dominated my social engagements. Late one summer evening, a stunning—I'm going to say it—knockout blonde with a sleeve tattoo grabbed me by the belt loop, pulled me to the bar, and yelled, "Come on, this one's on me." Still licking the wounds of my breakup just six months before, I was hellbent on finding anything or anyone who could fill the emptiness within me.

If ever there was a woman who was less like me, here she was. Her nose ring screamed danger, her hips peeking out of low-rise jeans actually moved to the music, and her Julia Roberts smile radiated throughout the exposed-brick basement of the dingy club. As we waded our way through the secondhand mist of excessive bro cologne vying for the bartender's attention, she looked in my eyes and ran her fingers through my hair.

"You're adorable. What's your name?" she screamed above the latest stupidly catchy party anthem.

I stared at her blankly. Shoot. What *was* my name?!

She gave me a side-eye and said, "Okay, Mr. Mysterious, I'll call you Alex."

Truthfully, I don't know what this girl saw in me. Perhaps safety in a room full of aggressive drunks. Innocence, maybe? Or possibly she had a thing for tall, baby-faced music teachers. Whatever fueled her passion, she quickly placed an overfilled blue swirly shot into my hand and guided my wrist to the sky. She pulled me close to her face and shouted to the ceiling, "To forgetting who we are!" The crowd cheered in recognition of our collective binge-drinking goal.

As the sweet alcohol burned the back of my throat, the edges of the room did something I'd never experienced. They moved from blurry to completely in focus as if the eye doctor had switched the buttons on the vision checker machine. In a bit of a daze, I rubbed my palms against my eyeballs. Despite taking a double shot, I was actually sobering up as the words of her proclamation rang in my ears. *Is this all life is? Forgetting who we are?*

The night tore on. The girl with the sleeve tattoo shook her butt against my body for seven or eight more songs. When her friends hollered to leave, she took my phone and quickly entered her number. She leaned into my ear and whispered once more, "To forgetting who we are."

Then she disappeared into the night.

The next morning, I woke up nauseous and aching on a friend's overstuffed and sagging sofa, my excessively long legs dangling over its beige, crusty armrest. I looked at the other four guys sprawled out around the room in various states of non-pregnancy-related morning sickness. Driving home, I smiled as my phone buzzed with a text from the nose ring herself. I saw the long texts I had no recollection of sending the night before.

As I rolled my windows down and cruised through the dusty 94 Tunnel, her tagline continued to haunt me. I stared at the iconic Basilica of St. Mary and the Minneapolis skyline to my right and finally began to realize what I had known since college but had never been brave enough to say out loud: this way of living was completely empty. This endless pursuit of a wild and crazy life was leading me toward death.

For the first time, I saw this beautiful girl and every other soul from the overcrowded bar for exactly what we were—desperate.

Desperate to climb into a shot glass to forget our real lives.

Desperate for hilarious "Can you believe he did that?" stories.

Desperate to feel something after a day of monotony and simple existence.

Desperate to be uninhibited and reckless for a few hours.

I am not here to tell you how to live your life. We all have almost certainly encountered voices ready to condemn any toe that sneaks outside the line. Too often I've encountered strangers who attack a "sinful lifestyle" without ever attempting to understand those of us that have struggled beyond belief. Nobody, including me, asked why I was obsessed with getting wasted. My binge drinking was a symptom of loneliness, self-hatred, depression, and desperate attempts to numb the world away. I didn't need anyone to quote me a Bible verse about drunkenness. I needed someone to throw me a nonjudgmental life vest before I drowned.

I still like a highball of whiskey on a patio. I still support local breweries and distilleries. Heck, I will even occasionally pop into a club in Vegas (because I freaking love Las Vegas). But alcohol no longer controls me and never will again.

We all have times we get stuck in the wrong story. We get off track from who we were meant to be. You only get one time around on this crazy video game we call life. You are the main character; the controller is in your hands. You decide where your feet take you next.

I hope you're brave enough to change the areas of your world that feel dark and destructive. I hope you're bold enough to create a life you don't want to forget. I hope you're courageous enough to chase I-can't-believe-that-just-happened stories without alcohol. I hope you're strong enough to allow yourself to fully feel your emotions and fight for healing. I hope you never give up on a life that is fully and recklessly alive.

But most of all, if you've lost your way, I hope you never forget you can always choose a different path.

As my phone buzzed with a new text from Miss Dangerous, I silenced it and turned up the radio. *Oh, what I wouldn't give for a different life.* Wondering if I needed to puke again, I pulled into my driveway and looked up at my house. Would life always feel this empty and meaningless?

I rested my head on the steering wheel as a deep hopelessness settled in my unsettled stomach. My cell phone buzzed again, this time from the pack. "Guys, last night was epic! Same time next Friday?"

I looked at my face in the rearview mirror and for a second wished my heart would stop beating. "Bang," I said out loud, imagining a gun against my temple. I started to type, "I'm out next weekend, boys," but deleted it. I knew by next Friday I would be taking shots and trying to forget how much I hated every detail of my empty and miserable life.

CHAPTER 9

YOU CAN FIND ANOTHER WAY BESIDES SUICIDE

AGE 23

THE NIGHT FLEW BY like the cornfields around me. Ignoring any notion of a speed limit, I zoomed down the two-lane country highway, a dark and slippery road in the cold, late-autumn storm. The headlights were the only source of light other than an occasional agitated lightning bolt or passing vehicle. My car narrowly missed hitting a deer. I was racing as fast as I could from the torture that consumed every area of my young-adult life. My story mirrored King Midas's—only my touch turned things to pain and darkness rather than to gold.

"God, are you there?" I screamed at the roof of my car. "I want to die. If this is your plan for my life, you must really hate me!"

My brain began to loop its increasingly frequent mental-anguish montage. There I was—cowering under the seat on the school bus. Enduring repeated sexual assaults. Sitting in English class while a girl yelled, "Are you gay yet?" and everyone laughed. Withstanding hateful words from my voice teacher. Overhearing a bridesmaid tell her friends I was disgusting. Breaking up with the one girl I'd ever loved.

There I was year after year crying myself to sleep because I couldn't take it anymore.

The car clock read 2:36 a.m. I stopped to fill my tank at a ghost town of a gas station that looked like a cold-case crime scene waiting to happen. I had no idea where I was or how to return to the Twin Cities. Maybe I would never go back. Maybe I would move far away where nobody would know me or notice if I disappeared. *I bet Guam is nice this time of year.*

The tank clicked full, and I gave up on the grand entrance of a gas station axe murderer. I took the opposite on-ramp and headed back the way I had come. Off in the distance, two minuscule headlights appeared in the oncoming lane. As the truck grew closer, I prayed it would swerve over the dotted line and annihilate me. I stared into the passing driver's eyes and waited for the impact, but, like all the other vehicles that night, the semi zoomed past, sending a wave of water over my windshield and leaving me with another unanswered prayer.

With each passing mile marker, my mind fixated on its ever-increasing favorite topics: the easiest way to kill myself, cause an accidental death, or disappear entirely. Over the course of the past few months, those thoughts had slowly morphed from *what if*, to *maybe*, to—for the first time—*when*.

The road curved sharply, and one of Minnesota's 11,842 lakes came into view. I screeched into a small parking lot at the water's edge and wept from my soul. Looking at the notebook beside me, I furiously wrote everything I was feeling. The pen took on a life of its own. After five pages, I began to see the only choice I had: suicide.

You've thought about ending it for almost ten years. It's time to make a decision. Choose a day and get this over with.

I stepped out of the car and wandered down by the woods to take a leak when something across the water caught my attention. I pulled up my zipper and plopped down on a bed of rocks. I pondered a one-way swim to the middle of the lake. *Why don't I just end this right now?* Then, looking out at the cloud-covered waters, a strange peace and excitement took hold. I accepted my decision.

On December 25, I will either kill myself or never think about suicide again.

Depression is a crazy beast. Unless you've experienced its long midnights, it's hard to convey how warped the mind gets. Like people struggling with anorexia who look at their bodies wasting away and see themselves as fat, so, too, the mind becomes distorted beyond recognition. When I was growing up, no one ever talked to me about mental health or suicidal thoughts. No one stood up in front of me and said, "I almost killed myself when I was your age, but life got way better. You might not see it now, but your life will always have hope and a future."[14]

I've heard countless people say suicide is the most selfish decision on the planet. Although losing someone that way certainly is a loss unlike any other, imagine a pain so tormenting you wouldn't care what happened to your family and friends—you would endure anything to make it stop. If you could feel even for a few minutes the hell I was in during those months, I don't think you'd say I was selfish. I think you'd say, "I get it."

I know how alluring suicide's fake promise of peace sounds, because I've lived it more times than anyone should have to. I also know that voice presents a false choice as it whispers, "Suicide is your only choice if you want to be free."

If you woke up today believing that suicide is your best option, you are wrong. You have a million other options. You can choose:

To ask for help.

To fight for the healing and wholeness you deserve.

To call your doctor and talk about what you're going through.

To learn how nutrition, sleep, and exercise can improve your mental health.

To make an appointment with a counselor and open up.

To let go of toxic people.

To set boundaries around anyone who makes you want to die.

To fight back against the endless automatic thoughts that scream you are worthless.

To believe, against all odds, that tomorrow will be better than today.

Do not spend another hour suffering in silence. Do not spend another minute being a victim in your own life. Do not spend another second believing the God of the universe has abandoned you. Depression is not a choice. Suicidal thoughts are not a choice. The abuse, trauma, and struggle you have been through were not a choice. But death is not your only way out.

I promise you can find another way.

———

I pulled into my cracked and weathered driveway; the clock read 5:21 a.m. The darkness outside the car mirrored the darkness within my crumbling heart. I looked at the notebook on the passenger's seat beside me and saw the scribbled words in my journal from the hours before.

On December 25, I will either end my life or never think about suicide again.

I quietly entered the front door, snuck into my bedroom, and collapsed. Lacking the energy to take off my street clothes, I sunk into my old, lumpy mattress and gave into the only other way I could escape the agony: I slept.

CHAPTER 10

YOU CAN CHANGE THE ENDING

AGE 23

I DIDN'T GRAB THE life vest as I left. No part of me wanted to be saved. I began swimming out past the buoys to the drop-offs where I'd been warned never to go. As I raced into deeper waters, the gentle sand that held the foundation of my existence gave way to new ground, a place of ragged depths and jagged glass. I continued to move out to sea. My bleeding feet stung and cramped in the glacial waters. Soon the waves crashed above my head, pushing me back toward shore in an attempt to spit me out of the ocean's mouth. Still, I moved toward oblivion—for oblivion was the sole reason I had come.

I pressed on with efficient and powerful strokes until the beach was a mere pencil line on the horizon behind me. At any moment the undercurrent could make its unpredictable appearance, forcing my hand and seizing any chance to change my mind. I paused, treaded water, and stared into the vast indifference on all sides. Despite the cold settling deep in my bones, I heard Poseidon beckon me even further into the heart of the sea. For a moment I thought I heard a faint voice calling out above the dissonant, aquatic melody that was quickly becoming my life's benediction song. I spun around, searching in all directions, but nothing came into view. *Who would care enough to save me? It would be weeks before anyone noticed I was missing. No one could reach me in time now even if they knew where I had purposefully wandered.*

The turbulence of the tide ferociously splashed and tossed me as I swam, while the lactic acid burned through my exhausted limbs. With the waves towering four feet above my head, I stopped kicking and allowed my body to be pulled under. It would all be over soon.

Beneath the surface, I opened my eyes in a last-ditch effort to glimpse any sign of hope above. Disoriented, my vision stung in the blur of salt water. Pitch-dark, murky depths greeted me. I slammed my eyes closed again, only wanting the pain to subside, and sent up a desperate prayer for the end to quickly arrive. Unlike the thrashing above, the waves were less powerful beneath the surface, their movement a mere nudge. The watery ceiling above grew farther from me as I willingly slipped away.

I tried to calm the agonizing desperation in my lungs when a long-lost feeling started to take hold deep in my soul like a familiar hymn echoing in a stained-glass sanctuary. Strangely, it was almost identical to the longing that had lured me out into the open waters in the first place which promised the pain could all finally stop—the elusive peace I had dreamed of for more than a decade.

Just then, a dark figure started floating toward me. Startled, I immediately recognized this old acquaintance who had tried to visit so many times in the bathroom, knife in hand. Death was swimming closer and closer into view. An explosion of pain rattled within my chest as my body—frantic for any morsel of oxygen—sent out an S.O.S. Was this truly the end, the moment when I would finally surrender to the darkness once and for all? Would the happy ending I'd desired become the "alternative ending" no one would ever see?

A dormant survival instinct arose within me, overriding control of my arms, and shockingly launched my torso back above the surface. My entire body shook as coughs of water poured out of my mouth and full-on panic set in. I glanced at the distant shore. Seagulls circled above, cheering on my demise like a gladiator in the Roman Colosseum. Collapsing in exhaustion, my head sank beneath the surface one last time as my body folded in half, taking its final bow. Then my eyes flew open; I wanted to make a different choice. I wanted to live. I opened my mouth to scream for help, but my voice merely mumbled in the water. I had no strength left to change my mind. No one could hear my cries for a second chance. Reaching for the surface, I began falling faster and faster, as if being sucked through a black hole.

I burst upright in my bed, sweat pouring off my forehead and blood pulsating through my veins. Gasping for air, I looked around at the darkness in my room. I touched my face to confirm I was still alive. The dream had felt so real. The weapons I planned to use hid within the solid oak dresser drawers, waiting expectantly among a sea of socks and boxer shorts.

I began reliving the dream's vivid moment. Was I making the right choice? What if, during the act, I wanted to change my mind?

I closed my eyes, desperately wanting to pass out without getting sucked into another night of my inner demons pounding me into the ground. Soon, however, the ticker tape started scrolling through my brain.

The world would be much better off without you.

People merely tolerate you.

You're doing them a favor by not having to put up with you.

Maybe a gun would be better?

You'll never get married. Who would ever marry someone so repulsive and worthless?

Isn't it obvious why no one ever stays in your life?

I clenched a pillow, pressed it around my face and over both ears, and tried to silence the unspoken words. Right on cue, the most painful vignettes of my story kidnapped me into a spiral of self-destruction. Suddenly I was watching through the window of that small-town coffee shop. As the scene played out, I began screaming at my past self.

"Don't say it!"

In anguish, I rolled around my bed, but the scene didn't stop.

"I don't love you," I said.

I mentally pounded my fists on the glass. *Please, God. Change the ending. Change the ending.*

But the ending never changed. Only the reality of what I had done, what I had said, and the unbearable truth: she was gone forever.

She was your one chance at happiness.

She was the only person who cared to see your scars and love you anyway.

She was the best thing that ever happened to you, and you hurt her so badly.

There would be no sleep. I tried to think of anything else; however, the stupid dark room was inescapable now.

You're not a real man.

Nobody needs you here.

You'll always be alone in this world.

No one loves you, and no one ever will.

Why wait until Christmas? Let's get this over with tonight.

Of course she chose someone who is everything you're not.

Do you really want to be this miserable for the next sixty years?

Friends? What friends? Who has shown up when you needed them the most?

You've been plotting this for weeks. No one cares about you enough to notice.

You're already invisible to 99.999 percent of the world. What's the difference?

I barely lifted myself off my mattress, tripped, and fell against the dresser. I opened the drawer and picked up the knife, unleashing it from its leather cage. The sharp edge seemed to release a villainous laugh as the light reflected and moved across the wall. Without breaking the skin, I gently pressed the blade against the length of my wrist, flirting with a rush of power and danger.

I had approached this moment so many times before—skating at the brink of death but never strong enough to complete the act.

You could show them all right now.

They were right about you. A wuss. An ugly nobody.

You could get them back for every horrible thing they've ever said and done.

Too exhausted to put the case back on, I set the knife down and plummeted facedown into bed. I pulled the string on the bedside light. The pillow muffled the sobs that convulsed from my stomach as I listened to the accusing voice.

Don't you just want it all to stop?

No one's coming to change the ending.

Tomorrow this will all finally be over.

CHAPTER 11

YOU CAN CHOOSE TO STAY

AGE 23

MY EYELIDS BARELY OPENED before I slammed them shut and rolled over. Through the haze of confusion and the daily morning resentment, my mind finally realized what day it was—Christmas. Yes, today was so much more important than underdog reindeers and eggnog hangovers. Not only was it the historically inaccurate birthday of the Savior of the world, today I would make the single most dire decision of my entire life: whether I wanted to stay alive or finally be free from the pain.

Christmas had snuck up on me. Not in its usual busyness of holiday parties, cookie baking extravaganzas, white-elephant gift exchanges, and tracking down loved ones' lists of consumerist desires. No, weeks of preparation had flown off the calendar because of my obsession with making sure every suicidal duck was in its row. More than a decade of hating myself, burying my story, and cringing at my reflection in the mirror had been bottled up under intense pressure, and today it would finally explode. Despite the imminence of the day's events, I remained lifeless in my bed like it was a normal, lazy Sunday.

Forty-five minutes later, my mind refused to settle back into unconsciousness, so I waved my white flag and accepted the disgusting reality of being awake. Despite my meticulous planning, there were still too many variables. Like what if I wanted to change my mind?

Fear of the excruciating pain clenched in my stomach as I lay spread out in my bed like a blanket-covered starfish. Despite my nervousness, the possibility of it all being over excited me. I craved death. All I wanted was a new existence—to be reincarnated as someone attractive and desirable. I wanted to come back as the life of the party. The guy everybody adores, with loads of money and a head-turning ride—so basically a rich underwear model. My reflection in the six-dollar college dorm mirror confirmed I didn't deserve to be alive.

I fell back on the bed, my hands cradling the back of my skull while the day's first tears began to puddle in my eyes. The illness of depression had wreaked havoc on every area of my life, making even the most basic functions—such as eating and sleeping—seem impossible. Some days I would eat an entire box of Oreo cookies with a quart of ice cream and then a whole bag of Spicy Nacho Doritos. Other times

I would miss meals for days as if I were on a hunger strike. Some nights the deafening voices in my head left me with a self-hate-fueled insomnia. Other times, you couldn't lift me out of bed with a construction crane for three days in a row. Some mornings I woke up feeling stronger, but while out with friends I would succumb to a panic attack and need to escape as soon as possible.

I imagined the frenzied disbelief that would spread from circle to circle tomorrow. I couldn't wait for so many cruel humans to think, "Maybe I shouldn't have been such a jerk to him." I wanted them to suffer. But not my family and friends. They were the innocent bystanders caught in the cross fire of a life that never should have existed. They were the true casualty of it all.

I didn't want to go through the actual act of dying. I would have given anything if Will Smith would have shown up to do his *Men in Black* thing, flashing everyone with his fancy bright white light and erasing any memory of me. But, like my life as an underwear model, this was never going to happen. The choice was bigger than to live or die. It was the choice between a lifetime of eternal pain or a few minutes of extreme pain and eternal peace.

I opened the second-to-bottom drawer of my dresser and pulled out the supplies. I stared down at the blue veins protruding from my forearm waiting for what was to come. I glanced at a few belongings stacked in brown boxes in my closet and the pile of addressed and stamped envelopes. I ripped a piece of Scotch tape from my desk drawer and walked to the bathroom door to attach my pre-written note:

Do not enter. Call 911.

I locked the bathroom door behind me and placed my supplies on the counter. Everything was ready for my final scene. Kneeling beside the toilet, I slid the dull side of the blade across my forearm without cutting the skin, just as I had so many times before.

Do it, wuss.

After a few false starts, I slammed the knife down on the counter and walked back to my room. I dove into bed, screaming and writhing in the sheer agony of this moment, the real ninth circle of hell. Desperate to drown out the abusive voices in my brain, I turned on the TV.

In one last plea for help, I prayed for someone to save me. I waited for my cell phone to vibrate with proof that someone cared, yet it remained still. I listened for a knock on the door, a stranger who just happened to know something was gravely wrong inside, yet no sound reverberated from the stairs below. I pleaded for someone—anyone—to wrap their arms around me as I cried uncontrollably, yet I was completely alone. After a few more hours of waiting, it became clear that no one was coming to rescue me.

I rose out of bed and sprinted back to the bathroom. In a surge of energy, I picked up the knife and pressed it harder against my wrist. *Come on, you pansy.* My breath grew heavy. *You aren't even man enough to do this, are you?* My foot stumbled. My head felt light and queasy. Unable to force myself to break the skin, I cried out in exasperation.

Gasping for air between heavy sobs, I threw the knife down on the ground and rocked back and forth in a fetal position. I ripped off my tear-soaked shirt and stood before the large vanity mirror. Horror-stricken at the sight of my reflection, I didn't even recognize the man staring back at me. With a demon-possessed look in my eyes, I put both hands on the counter in front of me as complete darkness overtook the last inches of my lifeless body.

I repeated patterns of pacing, looking at the weapons, and collapsing to the floor. I reached for a towel and pulled it over me like a precious baby blanket. In and out of consciousness, I carried on for hours in this same tormented cycle.

You have failed at everything in your life; you can't fail at this, too. Are you too stupid to get this right? I pushed myself up from the ground and looked into my reddened eyes that screamed with intent to kill. *This is it—now or never.*

I picked up the knife for the last time. I moved back in front of the mirror and started counting backward from ten.

10 . . .

9 . . .

Images of my friends and family flashed through my mind—everything good I was choosing to leave behind.

8 . . .

7 . . .

Then I saw images of the worst moments—everything I would finally be free from.

6 . . .

I'm so sorry, everyone. I am so sorry.

5 . . .

Man up.

4 . . .

3 . . .

2 . . .

I gripped the knife tightly, just breaking the edge of the skin when a voice broke through.

Have you really given life everything you've got?

If you have, give up. Go ahead. End it.

But I don't think you have.

This is the easy way out.

I think there is more in you.

I froze, looking at little drops of blood from the Band-Aid-sized cut where the knife had started but not finished. *Have you really given life everything you've got? Have you really done everything you can to fight back? Have you really gone after becoming the man you've always wanted to be?*

I blinked. The question repeated again and again.

Have you really given life everything you've got?

My body awoke from a deep, menacing trance. I cleaned up my surroundings, raced out of the room, and ripped the warning sign off the bathroom door. I shoved any trace of the day's events into my backpack and snatched up the stack of stamped goodbye letters. I threw on my coat, forced my feet into a worn-out pair of tennis shoes, and rushed out into the cold. Sliding into my car, I flung the backpack onto the passenger's seat and tore out of the driveway. My tires screeched as I shifted into drive, accelerating away from that bathroom as fast as humanly possible.

With each passing mile, the mind-controlling emotions slowly subsided and clarity began to emerge. Was I really choosing to stay?

I sincerely hope that life never hits you so hard you wonder if it's worth living. I hope you never feel what it's like to be locked in the dark room of depression with its stench of failure and wallpaper of scars. I hope you never get to a place so desperate you're counting backward from ten.

When I was a kid, I remember hearing stories in Sunday school about miracles. I always wanted to see one. After a while, though, I kind of gave up. I bought into the "God used to do cool things but doesn't anymore" philosophy and went about my life. But now I see I was looking for miracles in the wrong places. I still think God can do, and, indeed, does inexplicable wonders in the world, but I also know some of His greatest miracles are done in the hearts of broken people. The fact that you've gone through so much and are still standing is miraculous.

God has always been in the business of miracles. Creating the world from nothing. Saving his children from impossible circumstances. Bringing people back from the dead. While I may never see anyone turn five Hostess Twinkies into five thousand, I now know that the miracle I always wanted to see happened within me. I am a living, breathing miracle. And so are you.

God sent his son Jesus into the world to show us how to be recklessly alive. During His time here, Jesus gave everything He had to help people escape their own darkness. He gave everything He had to spread truth and attack the legalistic, oppressive voices. He gave everything He had to teach us how to love and help people who can never repay us.

For everything Jesus gave, the people who once cheered His name called for Him to be publicly tortured and nailed to a cross through His hands and feet. He died the most painful of deaths so that we could live. Throughout His life and death, God was saying to us, "I will give everything I've got—including sacrificing My one and only son—so that, if you believe, you will never perish, but have eternal life."[15]

My suicide attempt taught me that God is not just talking about an eternal life in heaven, but a full life that is available to us every second we are alive.

Whatever hell you face in this lifetime, never forget that you have a choice.

Choose to find your purpose and never give up on making the world a better place.

Choose to own your story and stop hiding the real chapters that make you who you are.

Choose to keep clawing out of the stupid dark room and ask for the help you deserve.

Choose to do whatever it takes to make it through the sh*t.

Choose to combat any abusive voice that gets in your way.

Choose to forgive yourself for the pain you've caused.

Choose to pave a different path when you get stuck in the wrong story.

Choose to find another way besides suicide.

Choose to give life everything you've got.

Choose to stay.

Late in the evening I pulled into an abandoned parking lot in downtown Minneapolis and sat alone in the silence of my heated car. *Merry Christmas, Sam.* I watched as the green minutes ticked by on my digital car clock.

11:57
11:58
11:59
12:00

I had made it. I had decided to stay.

Reversing out of my parking space, I drove back into the world I'd planned to leave behind. I merged onto the overlit city highway with the goodbye letters still in the backpack beside me. Taking an exit to an industrial park, I ripped each envelope into little pieces and chucked them into a dumpster as tall as I was.

Pulling back into my driveway, I looked up at the bathroom window and imagined how different this moment could have been. Police cars' swirling blue lights surrounding my house. Devastated family members cradling their heads. Weeping friends huddled on the curb. First responders loading my body into the back of an ambulance.

I entered the house, walked past the bathroom door, and stepped into my tidy room. For the first time in weeks, I didn't hear the loops of self-hate. Instead, I felt peace I'd been searching for all day. Within minutes, I was asleep—safe from the Christmas nightmare that had almost come to pass.

PART THREE

CHAPTER 12

YOU WERE MADE TO JUMP

AGE 24

IT WAS THE TYPE of winter day when people decide once and for all to move south. A cloudless sky teased the world below, while a negative four–degree temperature encouraged normal people to hibernate indoors. There I was, haphazardly dressed like a homeless Eskimo and fastened to a strange, large man who smelled of Axe body spray and beef jerky. From behind my robbery-approved winter mask, I stared out of an open plane door 12,500 feet above the desolate snow-covered cornfields of Nowheresville, Minnesota, and began to panic.

Barely thirteen months after my planned suicide attempt, I—the terrified, never-take-risks guy—purchased a ticket to . . . skydive. Who was this new man looking back at me in the rearview mirror? What miracle had taken place for this human to attempt such a dangerous and un-Sam-like feat?

A few days after the attempt, I made a reckless decision. I would do one thing every day to make my life better or make the world a better place. And photograph it. No skipping days. No excuses. It was time to take my life back.

On December 30, I hopped in the car and drove seven hours to southern Iowa to spend a weekend ringing in the New Year with two close college friends instead of staying home and throwing myself a black-tie pity party. The road trip and time spent with people who loved me immediately boosted both my mood and my will to live.

The first week of January, I organized my room, made plans with a friend I hadn't seen in a long time, cooked a new recipe for my mom, and donated blood. Even when I didn't feel like it emotionally, I forced myself to take action.

> Day 11: Researched my genealogy
> Day 12: Planned a trivia night with high school friends
> Day 15: Volunteered to clean at a women's shelter
> Day 17: Donated two boxes of used clothes
> Day 22: Wrote a song for my fifth- and sixth-grade Sunday school kids
> Day 24: Scraped old wallpaper at my mom's house
> Day 26: Volunteered with Meals for Minds, a project that provides food for kids at inner-city schools
> Day 31: Took my first painting class

Day 39: Created a bucket list

Anytime the lies in my brain tried to convince me things would never get better, I opened the photo album and saw visual proof of people who loved me, memories of why I wanted to be alive, and the positive impact my life was having on the world around me. I posted the photos online every night for over five months.

"Where are we? Is this even a real street?" my best friend Dan said. As we turned down a dirt road, the GPS lady bellowed at us like I was her hearing-impaired husband.

"We could be murdered out here, and no one would ever find our bodies. Why are we doing this, again?" he asked.

These were all valid questions. Luckily, Dan was the sort of friend every person needs: kind, spontaneous, and crazy enough to go along with my occasional hair-brained schemes. We had purchased two coupons online for a discounted skydiving experience. Take it from me, skydiving is something for which you should willingly pay full price.

Turning into the parking lot of an outdated airport, the heightened concern for our imminent death still didn't deter us from continuing on with our quest to purposely fall from the sky. As we exited the car, the crisp January wind made yet another attempt to convince us to turn around and run for our lives.

Perhaps January in Minnesota isn't the ideal time to skydive.

A man with a dark beard halfway down his chest greeted us with zero emotion—like it was his thirtieth summer working the Tilt-A-Whirl at the county fair—and ushered us into a conference room. Sitting down in a faded, square-armed, antique chair, I looked around and imagined this being the place he would later inform our next of kin that we had plummeted to our deaths. After signing away our lives, an amateur VHS safety video magnified our concerns about the legitimacy of this organization. Dan and I were instructed to empty our pockets, put on a 1930s-looking leather football helmet, and slip into a harness.

Then, without any further discussion, we were climbing into a plane headed toward outer space.

The tiny aircraft barely fit four grown men plus a pilot. Upon starting the ignition, the engine puttered—evidently annoyed to be awoken on such a frigid day. I took inventory of the events thus far: A discounted ticket price. A dirt road leading to the middle of nowhere. A practically abandoned office building. Outdated leather helmets and well-worn harnesses.

Were we being too reckless?

The plane slowly ascended, and the ground became smaller and smaller as if we were looking down at a miniscule model of the world below. Dan raised his eyebrows at me to say without words for the hundredth time, "What have you gotten us into?"

Somewhere near the ozone layer, the plane leveled out and the large man motioned for me to stand and get ready. Crouching down in a plane designed for Keebler elves, he fastened himself behind me for our tandem jump. He gave the thumbs-up to another man, who slid open the door and looked down at his fingernails like he was working the checkout counter at the 7-Eleven.

"We're going to scoot up to the door, and you're going to put your foot on the metal leg so you don't hit your body on it when we jump. Got it?" I opened my mouth, but the terror of my impending death rendered my vocal cords paralyzed and silent. Somehow, I managed to nod. My knees knocked together, and I hesitantly extended one foot out of the airplane like the world's worst Space Force ballerina.

"Are you ready?" The man screamed with an intensity that made me think we were about to invade Nazi Germany.

"Is anyone ever *ready* to jump out of an airplane?" I hollered back. Apparently, when typed into Google Translate under "skydiver-ese," this means, "Yes, kind sir. I am physically, mentally, and emotionally prepared to jump."

Because then we were falling.

I think God, like any great parent, wants all of His kids to fall in love with being alive. To live for a purpose, to love deeply, and to help others however we can. It's easy to get tunnel vision and buy into the lie we only exist to seek comfort, pleasure, and the illusion of happiness. But everything I believed about how to be more alive changed when I stopped living for myself and started trying to be a little more like Jesus.

I'll be the first to admit there's a chance He wasn't talking about skydiving when He said that whole "I have come so they could have life, and have it to the fullest" thing.[16] Yet jumping out of an airplane was an outward sign of the healing God and I were fighting for—together. I still had dark days, but I was starting to internalize that my life was worth living.

I partially attribute that change to talking to my doctors, starting counseling, connecting to others who struggled with mental health, and learning new skills to help fight back when my brain became a scary place. But I also attribute the comeback to realizing almost everyone I was listening to had no idea how to live.[17] Instead of looking to the culture around me, for the first time I was looking to God.

I don't always know how to do that. I've felt like a church outcast for most of my life. There are so many confusing parts of the Bible and so many people who love screaming about them, I burn out on meaningless religion faster than a soaked log on a campfire. But maybe following God is more about being a disruptor, fighting injustice, spreading hope, and giving life everything you've got. Maybe following Jesus has nothing to do with the hate you give and everything to do with the love you show.

If you can't see that life is worth living, maybe it's time to change. Maybe it's time to explore the plethora of healing options available to you. Maybe it's time to stop caring what everyone thinks and instead care more about being the person you were created to be.

Please don't spend your whole life stuck inside the plane—bored and just trying to make it through the ride. If you feel lost and lifeless, it's because you weren't made to obsess about wealth, appearances, promotions, and popularity. You weren't made to sit back and watch everyone else do great things. You were made to be recklessly alive. You were made to jump.

Following a manly high-pitched shriek (I don't want to talk about it) and a few seconds of shock, I opened my eyes and took in a deep breath of fresh atmosphere. As we continued to free-fall, reality set in. I had jumped! My body tingled with adrenaline as arctic winds whooshed against the loose skin on my face.

The large man attached to my back pulled the parachute, and our falling slowed a bit. He calmly told me to start shaking side to side, which I assumed was totally normal. After a number of attempts to wiggle our bodies, he said, "Okay, we're going to free fall again."

"Awesome!" I shouted. The drop *was* the best part anyway.

After another fifteen seconds of uninhibited plummeting, our parachute again cranked open with a jolt. As we floated downward to the frozen fields below us, I wondered if Skydiver Man was always this on edge. We braced our legs for impact, falling backward and landing on top of each other as the parachute settled behind us. Soon after, Dan and his skydiving partner landed about thirty yards away. I ran and high-fived Dan, who informed me that my first parachute had been tangled, and his skydiver companion had screamed some colorful words as he watched our risky descent. If our second parachute hadn't opened, we wouldn't have survived.

"That's only the second time that's happened in eight years," my free-falling "expert" said to me, finally catching his breath.

In disbelief of my near-death experience, Dan and I rocked out to loud, celebratory music over the course of our drive home.

"So, same time tomorrow?" I said as we pulled into my driveway. Dan laughed and rolled his eyes.

I had jumped. And, thanks to a backup parachute, I was alive.

CHAPTER 13

YOU WERE MADE TO HEAL

AGE 24

I TAPPED THE GENERIC blue pen against the clipboard, mentally refusing to answer the weekly questions glaring up at me:

Over the last seven days, how often have you been bothered by the following problems?

1. Little interest or pleasure in doing things; feeling down, depressed, or hopeless
2. Trouble falling asleep, staying asleep, or sleeping too much
3. Feeling tired or having little energy
4. Poor appetite or overeating
5. Feeling that you're a failure or a disappointment to yourself or others

6. Trouble concentrating on things, such as reading the newspaper or watching television
7. Moving or speaking so slowly that other people could have noticed
8. Thoughts of hurting yourself or that you would be better off dead

Each answer I circled—not at all, several days, more than half the days, nearly every day—indicated the state of my somewhat-debilitating depression. While my counselor finished recording notes from his previous patient, my brain wrestled with a dilemma.

Early in my therapy journey, I learned that complete disclosure results in the possibility of being checked into a hospital, follow-up texts requiring me to lie and say I was not suicidal for documentation purposes, and ultimately paying for additional $125 sessions for even more scrutiny about the depths of darkness within my brain. Furthermore, providing honest feedback would lead to a barrage of probing questions.

"Where are you at with medication?"

"Should we go back to multiple sessions per week?"

"Do you think it's time to try outpatient therapy?"

"Do you want to be part of a trial at the university?"

"You sound lonely. Have you tried to make new friends?"

"Have you found trusted people you can talk to when you're feeling suicidal?"

"Which goals have you made progress on?"

Then, he would inevitably sigh, implying he, too, was frustrated with the glacial pace of my mental health recovery. So, for the umpteenth week in a row, I selected acceptable answers—enough to show I was still very depressed, but not to the point where he was obligated to freak out.

Counselor Man took the clipboard, calculated my score, and read his iPad for another thirty seconds before saying his usual: "Where would you like to begin today?"

I would like to run screaming from this room. I would like to not spend the next fifty-six minutes talking about my trauma and abuse. I would like to climb into bed and sleep for a few months.

Instead, I said, "Well, it's been an okay week."

I set an elbow on the armrest and leaned my head against a fist. My body language communicated clearly: *My defenses are up today. Don't push too hard, bubba.*

This counselor wasn't perfect, but at least there was a gentleness to his spirit that didn't send me nosediving through the second-story glass window beside us. I desperately wanted to quit, but he didn't give me a twenty-minute sermon (like counselor number one I'd stopped seeing) and wasn't obsessed with talking about sexual abuse (like counselor number two I'd stopped seeing), so I accepted that this deteriorating, serial-killer office complex was the best option. I had promised God I would give someone one year. A full year. An expensive year. An exhausting year. But, a full year of trying to heal as many broken chapters within me as possible.

He raised his eyebrows, cueing me to put the talk in this whole talk-therapy adventure we were on together, so I quickly started babbling about the ups and downs of the previous seven days.

"Last week, we talked about you writing a letter to him. Is that something you would like to read aloud and share with me today?" *No sir, I do not want to talk about him ever again. He is a cruel human, and I hope a mutant leech takes off his pinky toe and everyone starts calling him "Nine Toes McGee."*

"Um, sure," I said, opening my navy-blue therapy journal.

I proceeded to read what I'd scribbled on the page, my voice flat and detached from the emotion-filled words coming out of my reluctant mouth: "I am still trying to forgive you. For as long as I live, I will never understand how you could have claimed to love me and made that decision . . ."

After I finished, we both sat quietly, seemingly stunned by the raw pain I had released into the air.

"How did you feel while you were writing it?" he inquired.

Like driving to his house and slashing all of his tires. Like drinking half a handle of gin straight from the bottle. Like going to counseling is stupid and pointless and an expensive waste of time.

"It was pretty tough," I said.

He raised his eyebrows again, waiting for me to elaborate while I narrowed my eyes and dug my heels into the Tetris-patterned carpet. *Earth to Counselor Man, I have spent years building up walls and learning to disassociate from the worst days of my life. Like heck if I'm just going to let you tear them down with your eyebrow raising.*

Calling my bluff, he continued to wait. I peeked at the digital clock on the end table beside me. Forty-seven more minutes. Maybe jumping out the window wasn't such a bad plan after all.

"You are the type of patient I am most afraid of," he said later in the session. "With the life that you live, the accomplishments you've achieved, and the intense level at which you function, no one would ever guess what is actually happening inside of you."

Oh my gosh, what an enormous compliment. Or, wait, was that a giant burn? Am I going to need to slash your tires, too?

"The more you care, the better you get at hiding it," I said.

For a long time, we sat in silence, wrestling with the implications of both our words.

If I believed the stigma, I'd think counseling is only for crazy people. It was invented for those who don't have all their lights on, those who don't have friends who listen to them, anyone who thinks the earth is flat, or those who are convinced a Shel Silverstein poem is a telling of their own life.

If you haven't guessed, I was not the ideal candidate or spokesperson for talk therapy. I railed against it, hated most of it, and often scoured the internet for scientific data to prove my theory that spending money on a Caribbean vacation could have been equally—if not more—effective.

This is why I'm also the right person to tell you it changed my life. Nobody warned me before I started that things might get worse before they get better. Nobody told me that the benefits weren't always instantaneous but came to the surface over time. Nobody mentioned how there is no perfect path to healing, that it's mostly just a windy road of trial and error as you work at becoming a little more whole.

I hate when people say you'll feel better if you talk about it—mostly because I hate being wrong. While opening old wounds can be tough, I've also learned we tend to repeat the past until we repair it. Doing some hard work on myself and looking at ways I contributed to dysfunctional relationships freed me to try again without fear of the past. I realized, regardless of what some well-intentioned but misinformed churchgoers say, you can have a therapist and also love Jesus. I discovered there are a plethora of ways and opportunities to heal from mental illness, and having a point person to come back to over time is invaluable.

Healing requires action, my friend. It means making the phone call to get some help. It means letting someone help tear down your walls so you can finally start to feel alive again. It means you might not ever have to fight that battle alone. It means you can start to build a team that can help support you at your best and your worst.

I know life can feel hopeless, like there's so much pain a comeback isn't possible. But you're wrong. You weren't made to feel like crap for your whole life. You were made to heal.

"For next week, what do you think about writing a letter to yourself about this situation?" my counselor said.

That's stupid. I think you're just giving me homework so you can write something down on your fancy iPad. I think maybe next week I'll move to Guam.

"Yeah, I can try that," I said.

I threw my backpack in the trunk and slid behind the wheel. Starting the engine, I cradled my head in my hands and tried to shake the past hour's emotions out of my brain. I pulled into a swanky grocery store—the same store I'd worked at during all of my teenage years. I walked past the infamous salad bar floor toward the sushi case and selected a salmon roll for my weekly post-therapy self-care ritual. I stepped up to the cash register, but nobody was around. Looking at the maintenance closet door, I thought of the many hours I'd spent there a decade earlier and began to wonder how different my life could have been if I'd started counseling back then.

A lady with gray streaks in her black hair rushed around the corner, arms flailing to signify her apology for making me wait. After a moment, we both recognized each other—she was still working there long after I'd quit.

"Oh my gosh, how are you?" she asked.

Hungry. Depressed. Somewhat suicidal.

"I'm doing pretty good. How are you?" I lied.

"Did you end up marrying that bagger girl you liked?" she inquired.

"No," I chuckled. "But we're still friends."

I grabbed my receipt and exited the main door, just as I had after every grueling shift.

The deeper emotions of the counseling session began to fade as I drove home. Despite the ongoing turmoil in my brain, I didn't feel the need for an all-night drive because I had a weekly outlet for my struggles. Despite the intense emotions, I didn't need to hide and isolate because, as uncomfortable as opening up was, I knew I wasn't alone in this fight. Despite occasionally still slipping into the stupid dark room, I now had tools to get out faster than ever. Despite still wishing to no longer be alive from time to time, I knew I couldn't believe everything my mind was telling me.

Another week of therapy closer to completing my year. Another week of getting through it. Another week of doing the hard work needed to learn how to be more recklessly alive.

CHAPTER 14

YOU WERE MADE FOR ADVENTURE

AGE 24

"OUCH! OUCH!" OUR YOUTH leader, Uncle Sharky, called out while our ten-passenger van flew through the air and bottomed out in a crater-sized pothole, jostling everything and everyone inside. The previous night, our crew of sixteen had napped at a campground for a few hours before waking up at 3:00 a.m. to head for another day of performing music concerts at rural schools across the beautiful Zimbabwean countryside.

Despite being I-just-gave-birth exhausted (what do you mean men aren't allowed to use that phrase?), I couldn't sleep. Three weeks into the trip, I kept pinching myself to make sure I wasn't dreaming. Only eighteen months earlier, I had survived my harrowing day in the bathroom, and now here I was—barreling through Africa.

I gazed out the large van window—a van filled with people who had given up most of their summer to share in a faraway country about how a man named Jesus could change a person's life. A large pack of baboons stood on the side of the road either ready to sell me lemonade or hijack our van and take it for a joyride. My right arm was completely numb under the weight of one of my sleeping teammates. Local-radio worship music, accompanied by light snoring and the rustling of shifting sleepers, created a beautiful missionary's soundtrack.

After the sunrise, the van turned off the main two-lane drive onto a dusty dirt road and passed a small village of circular clay huts with thatched roofs. We pulled up to a closed gate at the entrance to the school, which was surrounded by large, rolling hills and located near the Zambia border. Filing out of the van, we Americans and the local dance team traveling with us exchanged yawns and hugs. I couldn't believe I was a part of this special makeshift family.

Back in Minnesota seven months earlier, a different secret plan had brewed in my stomach after my attempt; I would apply to spend my summer as a music missionary. As I stared at the acceptance letter on the same computer I'd used to write my goodbye letters, the floor-length list of obstacles set off earsplitting fire alarms in my brain. The biggest of all: fundraising $4,485—more than double what I made in a month as a young public-school teacher.

Not to mention I still had massive student loan debts. I hurled up excuses at God, but whenever I prayed I felt peace that everything would be okay. This trip could be the start of the reckless, adventure-filled life I had always wanted to live.

Once my plan became public, however, I faced backlash on all sides.

"What happens if you don't raise all the money? Can you afford that?"

Well, no—not really.

"Wouldn't you rather spend your summer drinking at the lake?"

Now that you mention it, that does sound quite nice.

"What are you going to do if you get malaria? Or HIV? Or both?"

Um . . . die, I guess.

I worked my tail off traveling to three states to lead worship and speak about this crazy mission I was on. I spent hours sending out support letters and making goofy fundraising videos. Slowly and faithfully, every vaccination and dollar fell into place.

We set up our PA system for a concert in the courtyard under the blistering sun. Hundreds of schoolchildren in their maroon and white uniforms crowded around our stage like we were the Beatles invading America. With all of the cables laid and our sound check complete, it was showtime. The other three vocalists and I burst onto the stage, jumping and dancing to our opening: "Tambira Jehovah!"

I hadn't sung in public since my senior recital; my voice teacher's damaging words still held hostage the music in my soul. But not anymore. Instead of moping around and wishing to be someone else, I was finally taking huge risks and meeting incredible people from all over the world.

I know you're afraid. I know you doubt yourself. I know you have voices from your past that have destroyed your self-worth. You question this "good" God and His existence altogether. You're wondering if you have what it takes.

Maybe you've stopped dreaming and setting goals because you can't take one more letdown. Maybe you've stopped letting people in because you can't withstand one more heartbreak. Maybe you've stopped going after what you want most because you're terrified the next rock bottom might be your last.

My mental health has never been perfect. I struggled at times even in Africa. But following my attempt, I stopped being life's punching bag and finally hit back.

If you think God is just a bunch of rules and something you have to get through so you can watch football, I'm not sure you really understand Him. I'm afraid His message of radical empathy and His invitations to wild adventures have been watered down by well-intended people trying to make a reckless God palatable for the comfort-seeking masses.

If you want to know if God is real, go on an adventure. Stare into the eyes of a woman who has no earthly possessions but has more hope than you can ever imagine. Make a decision to pursue your dreams no matter how much backlash you face. Read stories about the work Jesus did, and then get off the couch and create a life with amazing tales of your own.

You weren't made to pay bills and die.

You weren't made to sit inside and stare at a screen.

You were made for adventure.

———

After the concert, Uncle Sharky had a surprise. He was taking us to see Victoria Falls. The world's largest sheet of falling water—one of the seven natural wonders of the world—stands 5,604 feet wide and 354 feet tall.

We dashed to the entrance—past dozens of street vendors selling old trillion-dollar Zimbabwe bills. Racing down the narrow path, we pushed tropical branches out of the way. The sounds of the rushing water grew deafening. Large groups of bone-soaked tourists, wearing hurricane-worthy rain gear and clenching waterproof cameras, passed us going in the opposite direction.

Then, in a small opening in front of me, my eyes beheld the most amazing thing I had ever seen—Victoria Falls. Like Narcissus staring at his reflection, I could have stared at the falls until I starved to death. Our team snapped pictures and danced around in wild excitement, but I began to cry. (As if there weren't enough water around us already.) My beloved teammates noticed my tears, and a few of them wrapped their arms around me. I could only think about how I almost missed this.

How could I have believed there wouldn't be another single moment worth living? Sitting alone in that bathroom, I had no clue about the incredible adventures ahead, and now I couldn't be more thankful I had survived to experience them.

CHAPTER 15

YOU WERE MADE TO RISE

AGE 25

"SAM, WE HAVE TO do this!"

"Absolutely not," I retorted, crossing my arms in the bunk below.

"Come on, we're totally doing this."

"You couldn't pay me to do that in a million years," I said, standing my ground.

"Seriously, Sam, this is happening."

After the suicide attempt, I had made a promise. If God was calling me to something, I would say yes—no questions asked. I didn't know what that meant, only that it seemed like a much better plan than following my own selfish and self-destructive tendencies. Soon, God's invitations poured through my fireplace like Harry Potter's letters to attend Hogwarts School of Witchcraft and

Wizardry after Uncle Vernon nailed the mail slot shut. Silly Uncle Vernon. One of the most beautiful envelopes that flew through my chimney was the call to mentor two seventh-grade boys at church. I instantly met God with excuses: I don't know enough about the Bible, I'm not cool enough, I don't have time for this. However, I had made a promise to God, so I reluctantly and recklessly said yes.

All of a sudden, I was spending two hours on Wednesday nights with two young guys who took my breath away with their pursuit to be fully alive. They were always running, always wrestling, always laughing. It was as contagious as a kindergarten pinkeye outbreak. From the moment the *yes* left my lips, I made an oath to never be the awkward parent-figure who sits on the sidelines and occasionally pays attention. If I was going to do this, I wouldn't hold back. If they climbed into the human bowling ball, I would roll next. If they wanted to play red belly rules in ping-pong, lift your shirt up, Sam, so you, too, can get whacked. If they wanted to jump into a Minnesota lake in the middle of winter . . . wait. What?

As a citizen of the Land of 10,000 Lakes, I must tell you, Minnesotans maximize their water surface area in all seasons. We fish and ski on our excessive bodies of water in both one hundred–and negative thirty–degree weather because the lake is our happy place—no matter what mood Mother Nature is in. This sunny winter day topped out at a brisk sixteen degrees, which prompted the directors of the camp to cut a hole in the ice and invite everyone to jump in the water for a dip. Because that's a normal idea.

"We're doing this," Ethan repeated on the second day of our winter youth group retreat.

Sometime between the broomball tournament and snow tubing, the worship band and the strange food–eating contests, the camp director announced the Polar Plunge would be taking place next to the dining hall, nachos would be served at 4:00 p.m., and a gray Cadillac had left its lights on.

"What in the world would possess anyone to be this insane? What's the point!" I yelled back.

Ethan met the statement with his teenage, stop-be-ing-ridiculous stare. You know the look. It's the same one you get when you ask him if he thinks he spends too much time with his phone.

"Are you going to jump with me or what? You're not scared, are you?"

Here it was—a test. Was I truly all in? Was I serious when I said I would do anything for these guys? I rubbed my eyes with my palms as a crazed roller coaster ride of butterflies crashed into the lining of my stomach. No part of me wanted to get in the water. I hate the cold. I hate everything about it. Then I had the terrible thought that has both ruined and saved my life: what would someone who was recklessly alive do? Blast. He would jump.

Outside the lodge, the massive crowd of appropriately bundled-up adults and teenagers surrounded the five-foot square hole in the ice just down the hill from the main lodge. Those of us who were experiencing a delusional state of lunacy and had decided to take the plunge formed an I'm-not-going-you-go group at the edge of the water.

The first kid emerged from his parka donning his Hawaiian-print swim trunks—a nice juxtaposition. I looked at Ethan, my mentee, as my eyes widened more than the hole in front of us. He smiled at me with an enormous this-is-going-to-be-epic grin. I began rethinking every possible life decision that had led me here. Several more of the crazies had plunged into the depths when Rope Man called for the next contestant. I couldn't feel my toes. I shivered uncontrollably. *What the spinach dip was I doing?*

I frantically pulled my feet out of my shoes and stripped to my gym shorts and thin, green long-sleeve T-shirt. I hobbled through the snow up to the ice hole and stared into the murky abyss below. Paul Bunyan tied the rope around my waist and gave me a glance that said, *It's your funeral.* The wooden ladder I would hypothetically use to climb out of the water stood a few feet away. Without hesitation, I closed my eyes, stepped off the edge, and crashed into the lake below.

The millisecond my body completely submerged, every cell of my being screamed. Time screeched to a halt, and every second felt like an hour. Thousands of little pins pricked each inch of my soaked skin. An arctic paralysis consumed my body as if I were floating in purgatory between the light above and the abyss below.

Each time my suicidal thoughts have come back, I've felt even more hopeless in the relapse. To climb out of the water when your body feels paralyzed is perhaps the hardest thing any of us will ever have to do.

To make matters worse, misguided humans say things like:

"Just get over it."

"Cheer up."

"Things aren't so bad."

Or, once you've been struggling for a while, you might hear:

"He's always having a bad year."

"Oh, he's in one of his moods again."

"It's best to just leave him alone."

No one would ever say these things if they'd been down there under the ice—if they knew what it felt like to be trapped in the darkness. When getting out of bed seems insurmountable, climbing up a ladder seems impossible. In depression's depths, I would have told you I was completely alone. I was screaming for God to cut the rope and let me go. But, somewhat annoyingly, God never did.

I want God's presence to feel like a physical hug or an audible voice telling me exactly what to do. However, I've never experienced Him this way. It's more like coming across the perfect person in the trenches—like the two women voice teachers who came to my rescue. It's more like finding the courage to clench your bat under the covers and defend your family. It's more like a wave of peace that washes over you sitting alone in the woods. It's more like a gentle call toward healing your past so you can be fully and recklessly alive.

No matter how many times life swings hard, you can find your way back to the surface. When the lies in your brain holler for you to give up, remember you always have access to a God who will never leave you—no matter how alone you feel. Stop making the safest choice and start making some freaking memories. You are strong enough to reach for the ladder and push yourself up—one rung at a time.

You weren't made to stay stuck in the frigid, lifeless waters. You were made to rise.

───────

"*Oh* my gosh, *Oh* my gosh, *Oh my gosh!*" I squealed in a squeaky voice. As the rope fell to the ground, I took one glance and Usain-bolted for the indoor lodge fifty feet up the hill. Our fun-loving youth pastor "hilariously" stood in my way, as I sprinted barefoot through the snow past the crowds of onlookers. Like a total-body dose of Novocain, I felt almost nothing as I raced to the great lodge of everlasting heat. Running faster than ever before, I pushed the door open with a swoosh and threw my body into the dining hall, leaving a puddle behind me as I rushed to the bathroom. Inside, I immediately stripped off my clothes and hugged my dry towel and sweats as if I had found the Holy Grail—a warm, fluffy, life-giving Holy Grail.

Twenty seconds later, the bathroom door whooshed open again and Ethan ran in. We started laughing uncontrollably. Even in dry clothes, our body temperatures were still that of a frozen, cold-blooded Komodo dragon. I wondered aloud if I would ever feel warm again. We grabbed our soaked belongings and scurried from the pine tree–wallpapered restroom to our home cabin. We clamored to open the door and leapt into our sleeping bags—our bodies convulsing from the combination of shivering and extreme laughter.

"Okay, that was awesome," I said from safely within my sleeping bag, fairly certain I would never, ever go outside again.

"See, aren't you glad I convinced you to jump?" Ethan said from the bunk above.

"Let's go with yes. Now I will always remember this day," I said, closing my eyes and thanking God for the warmth after rising once again from the cold depths below.

Thank you, God, for giving me the courage to be fully alive. I wrote in my journal. Lesson learned for the day: always make the choice that creates the best memory. I slid the pages back into my duffel bag as another group of guys came in and asked us to go skiing. No part of me wanted to leave the cabin, and I certainly didn't want to break my face on a pine tree.

"Let's go," I yelled, jumping out of my warm bed, ready to continue making the day as epic as possible.

CHAPTER 16

YOU WERE MADE TO LOVE

AGE 25

"SO, DO YOU, LIKE, even try to date?" an old acquaintance asked me, as the bride shoved cake in the groom's face right on cue. I unsuccessfully held back my eye roll. In a sea of former friends turned acquaintances, I felt more alone than ever.

If you've ever existed as a twenty-something unmarried person, you know exactly what I'm talking about. Wherever you go, people incessantly ask about your relationship status, attempt to set you up with their cat-obsessed, ugly stepsisters, and give you the sad head tilt, which we all know translates to, "Oh, poor you." They see being single as less than—a season of life to be pitied.

After a few more hours of torturous small talk, I moved toward the bathroom and instead took a hard right to the exit. Shoving my hands into my coat pockets, I fumbled for my keys, eager to get back to the fixer-upper home I'd recently purchased for a secluded bout of overeating and self-loathing. Although I'd gone almost two years without an active suicidal thought—such as thinking about methods or making a plan—I still had plenty of well-worn *I want to disappear* thought patterns that refused to ever fully dissipate.

Exiting through the revolving glass door, I gathered my bearings. My eye caught a dark corner of the building. A middle-aged man with a red beard sat huddled on a metal city bench, smoking the end of a bent cigarette. As I looked at him, he didn't make eye contact. Still, something tugged at my heart to say hello.

I'm not that person who strikes up conversations with strangers. Heck, sometimes I don't even like to talk to people I do know. *Just say hi.* I resisted the urge for a few more steps before finally muttering a quick "Hello." The man, seemingly surprised by my greeting, replied, "Oh hey, hey, how are you?"

With one simple "Hello," I met Bill.

Migrating to the bench next to him, I asked about his day. He was bundled up in a faded black winter coat and a clean patriotic hat. Crutches lay across his lap. Every few minutes a cocktail dress and heels passed by and stared at us, but after a while I hardly even noticed.

Bill had never owned a car or a home. He walked twenty to thirty miles a day in a city of 300,000 people. After we had been chatting for a bit, he said, "It has been days since anyone has talked to me." Bill had been suffering from homelessness since age sixteen and had been in and out of jail since age nineteen. Now, at the slick age of forty-seven, he suffered from depression and ADHD. He'd made mistakes, but who hasn't?

I walked with him a few blocks and asked if I could drive him anywhere. After I offered to pick him up so he wouldn't have to hobble up the parking ramp, he asked, "Are you scared to be seen with me?" It had never entered my mind.

We crossed the street at a sluggish pace and took the elevator up to the third level where I'd parked my silver Honda Accord. As Bill got in my car, he asked if I was nervous. "Absolutely not," I replied. We drove in the direction of the hip, happening part of Minneapolis lovingly referred to as Uptown, where he asked if I could drop him off at one of his hideouts located over ten miles from where we had met. *How would he ever have stumbled all that way?*

"Are you hungry? Can I get you a hot meal?" I said while merging through the downtown streets.

"I don't want to take advantage," he mumbled as he looked out the window.

"It's no problem. Are you sure?"

"Well, I could really go for a hot cup of coffee."

After a slight debate about the best cup of joe, he told me to take a quick left. "I want to show you something," he said as his eyes sparkled. We pulled up in front of a city mansion with large oak steps, granite stone covering, and landscaping like you wouldn't believe. "This is where I grew up. I used to play on those steps and wait for my dad to come home from the car dealership. It seems like yesterday."

As we entered McDonald's, the people around us were clearly uneasy. When I first looked at him, I wasn't even positive Bill was homeless. Now, however, in the light of the golden arches I could see his beard was a little scraggly, and the years of struggle showed heavy on his face. I ordered him a large coffee and a hamburger and filled my cup with some Hi-C Orange Lavaburst pop. Bill openly shared his life story. He told me about his past—about his many times in and out of different prisons and workhouses. During the second hour of our hangout, Bill leaned in and whispered, "I've gone twelve days without alcohol. It's the longest I can ever remember." I told him I was so proud and encouraged him to stay sober.

Our night ended up in what Bill has deemed the "finest park in Minneapolis." He was probably more qualified than anyone to give out that award. Tucked away in a neatly trimmed bush was a pizza box Bill had saved. He offered me a piece, but I graciously declined. I didn't want to take advantage of his hospitality.

"Do you have a girlfriend?" he inquired.

We shared some stories about losing love, and he told me not to worry about it. "Any girl would be lucky to hang out with someone who was cool as hell like you." Boy, did I need to hear that.

We talked a little bit about God. I asked if he believed in the Big Guy and if I could pray for him. I put my hand on his shoulder and asked God to strengthen and heal my new friend. Before I left for the night, we shook hands. He told me I was in his top seventy-five favorite people he had ever met. He said, "I love you," and I think he meant it. I gave him my phone number and told him I would buy him a cup of coffee anytime he was sober.

"Are you an angel?" he asked. I had wondered the same thing about him.

"What is the most alive you have ever felt?" I read the prompt written in the fancy weekend church retreat journal and thought hard in the half-full sanctuary. Moments of my life flashed before me like a lifetime achievement award montage: scenes of vacations and road trips, scenes of parties and cabin weekends, scenes of falling in love.

The montage abruptly switched to a different theme. Now I saw my long body stretched out on a bus floor trying to get one hour of sleep on the nonstop bus ride to New Orleans for Habitat for Humanity. I saw images of leading worship in Zimbabwe and riding in the back of a pickup truck on an African safari. I saw myself preaching for the first time at church in front of 2,000 people. I saw myself sitting on a deck talking about deep stuff with some of the high school guys from youth group. I saw Bill.

In that moment, everything I believed about living life to the fullest started changing. My reckless, I-can't-believe-that-just-happened moments weren't about how easy and carefree a day could be, but about helping others and loving people along the way.

Like that night at the wedding—and for most of the years preceding it—I had believed the perpetual lie that marriage is life's ultimate goal. While I still pray for this in my own story, it makes me wonder how much time we waste feeling sorry for ourselves and obsessively searching for "the one" instead of being open and present to the reckless adventures God has placed all around us.

Maybe it's time we all spend less time worrying about adhering to the cultural age expectations of engagement-marriage-house-puppy-baby and spend more time worrying about trying to embody His love to those around us here and now regardless of our relationship status.

We feel recklessly alive when we help others because we were created to love—not just at the altar, but every day we are alive.

Before I said good night to Bill, he made me promise I would listen to his favorite Rush album, *Hemispheres*, an epic record with tracks eighteen to twenty minutes long. "Make sure you listen to the first song," he insisted. "I think it's about you."

As I pulled into my heated garage, the door closed tightly behind me. I shut off the engine and shook my head. *Had I really spent the night hanging out with a homeless man?* I unfastened my cuff links, climbed into a sea of clean, white overstuffed pillows and blankets, and hit play on my sleek MacBook Pro. Immediately a rich electric guitar solo belted out of its speaker, and a haunting voice began to sing lyrics about finding food and shelter and living as brothers. Tears slid down my cheek as I thought about the beautiful night spent with an incredible new friend.

A few weeks later, pages of research articles and drafts for my thirty-page master's thesis covered every inch of the couch, table, and floor of my living room. Only a small walking path remained. I was in my crazed academia mode—pressed against a deadline to complete my degree while teaching full-time and working as a wedding DJ in order to graduate debt free. My ringtone started blaring, muffled and lost under one of the dozens of stacks surrounding me. Finally locating it, I glanced down to see "Unknown Number" with a Minneapolis area code. My heart leapt.

"Hello, this is Sam."

"Brother, it's Bill. Can you come pick me up at the park?"

"Be there in twenty minutes." I smiled as he hung up, then dropped everything and headed out the door.

I pulled up to the curb next to an old man sporting a different army hat and checkered jacket. His wide grin revealed a smile without many teeth. I raced around my car to open the door and help him get in. He'd finally ditched the crutches, but he still struggled to walk. As I closed his door and got back in the driver's side, I smiled and said, "Where to today, my friend?"

CHAPTER 17

YOU WERE MADE TO DO THE IMPOSSIBLE

AGE 26

A WOMAN WEARING A shiny turquoise polo shirt and khakis darted in front of me, placed her arm around my shoulder, and took in the current state of my failing body. The excruciating pain exploding from my legs proved worse than anything I had ever experienced, and agony puddled in my eyes. The early October temperature had unexpectedly plummeted to thirty-nine degrees, and I was drastically underdressed. Standing a few feet from mile twenty of the 2014 Twin Cities Marathon, I, racer number 6221, was waist deep in what runner-type people call "the wall," a magical place where your body starts shutting down and you mentally would rather do anything—including repeat the seventh-grade swimming unit—than take another bloody step.

"Do you want to ride on the golf cart and be done? It's nearby," she said, raising her eyebrows. I roughly translated her words to mean in true Minnesota passive-aggressive fashion that her professional medical opinion was this: I'm pretty sure you're dying.

Why did I ever think I could do this?

My life will always be a disappointment.

I have never and will never be athletic.

He was right; I run like a girl.

She continued to walk slowly beside me, supporting my weight. I placed my hands over my face and withheld an agonizing scream to the heavens. My chest shook between gasps of failure, while the reality of telling everyone I didn't make it induced an insane bout of nausea. To be fair, it might have just been my organs shutting down, but it was hard to tell at that point. I searched the crowd on either side of the street, looking for any familiar face to make this impossible decision for me. "What's your name?" she asked. The edges of my vision started to blur. "And date of birth?" she continued, as she guided me away from the running course.

Hundreds of better runners passed me on all sides. No one except the medic seemed to notice I existed. The pop-up medical tent housed only two beds, two large duffel bags marked with stitched red crosses, and the intensity of a level-three trauma unit. One old man, with what appeared to be a broken foot, writhed as a medical professional attempted to examine him. Nearby, a woman lying on the ground clenched her chest while several polo shirts huddled around her.

Close to the time of my suicide attempt, I had joined my local Life Time Fitness. On the day of my semirequired free personal training session, I cowered in my car, too afraid to walk through the glass doors. Locker rooms were my hell, jocks my biggest bullies, and sports my greatest embarrassment.

Desperate to flee this place I already despised, I pulled out of the parking spot. After moving into the exit lane, however, I slammed on the brakes, pounded my fist on the steering wheel, and headed back to the spot from which I'd departed. As I forced my new running shoes out of the car, a sweat-drenched man with a six-pack visible through his sleeveless compression shirt walked past me to his luxurious James Bond car.

Inside, I swiped my card at the check-in desk. A man with arms bigger than my head extended his palm for a handshake. He led me through a department store–sized maze of bizarre workout machines which closely resembled medieval torture devices.

"Let's do a test to see where you fall on this fitness chart, then I'll walk you through your lifting plan," the giant said while scribbling on his clipboard.

Just put me down for the same fitness level as the Marshmallow Man.

"Um, alright," I said instead.

Following sixty minutes of weight machines, I sat huddled over a small black trash can, while the sweet aroma of fresh vomit floated through the already pungent gym air. I wiped the lingering throw-up liquid from my face and caught the eyes of several steroid junkies sneering in my direction. I wanted to give up and die.

Much to my surprise, a few months later I signed up for the Get Lucky 5K. Shrugging off the St. Patrick's Day sexual innuendo, I agreed to run five kilometers while wearing a lime green bib with a box checked *single* or *taken* (because some sexy love connection might have happened on mile two when my face was purple and my armpits chafed). It took twenty-eight minutes and fifteen seconds for the finish line to finally pass beneath my toes. Before I could say "shin splints," my friend Katie had talked me into registering for a ten-mile race coming up in a few months. A couple years later, I signed up for the Twin Cities Marathon—like an idiot—and, for more than six months, dragged my feet through some variation of the following training plan.

Monday: Pedal a stationary bike for no apparent reason.

Tuesday: Run the number of miles that match the number of drinks I should be downing at an after-work happy hour.

Wednesday: Get up at 4:30 a.m. and run ten miles before work because I've completely lost my dang mind.

Thursday: Run in inclement weather and hate my life, probably.

Friday: Utilize weight-lifting torture devices instead of taking shots at the local watering hole.

Saturday: Log an excessively long run while eating gel packs that taste like feet.

Sunday: Swim and then hover my mouse over the "cancel marathon registration" button on my laptop before passing out in exhaustion—only to wake up and do it all over again.

For the most part, I kept up my training schedule for over six months. Hundreds of hours of hard work had led me to this one decision.

I looked into the compassionate eyes of the medic again. My mind came back to me as I sipped water from a cup she had provided. *She is offering you a way out—take it.* The digital race clock read three hours and thirty-one minutes. Even if I crawled to the end, I could finish before the six-hour cutoff.

If you want to know what it feels like to be suicidal, consider signing up for a marathon. Now there's a marketing strategy. The mental strength it takes to move forward through the hardest miles are the day-to-day reality of those who struggle to stay alive. They cannot see the way before them. They cannot imagine the euphoria waiting up ahead at the finish line. They cannot look into the future with a clear mind and comprehend the devastating effects their decision will have on their family and friends.

All they can feel is the pain. All they can see is the chaos around them. All they can hear are the voices telling them peace is on the other side of a weapon.

Learning to train through this terrible illness can be awful. Much of it will make you want to rip your insides out. You're going to have to fight like heck, make some reckless decisions to just go for it, and ask for help even when you don't want it, regardless of how you feel.

> You can speak God's truth to yourself: you are good, you are worthy, you are loved.

> You can believe Jesus when He said with God all things are possible.[18]

> You can overcome the lies in your brain.

> You are not powerless.

> You are not hopeless.

Sometimes I still hold my finisher's medal, the tangible proof of my long and difficult fight to take my life back. That heavy chunk of metal symbolizes one victory over the darkest nights. Every suicide survivor deserves a medal. Every human who knows what it feels like to be drowning in a pit of despair deserves thousands of screaming fans and a parade in his or her honor.

But no one talks about suicide. No one knows what to say or how to say it. So we, the survivors, need to take over the narrative and own our journey.

When we omit the darkest parts of our stories, we fail to show the world how strong and unstoppable we truly are.

When we never share about the long midnights of depression, we don't allow others to see how hard we are fighting to climb the ladder.

When we hide and edit the war that rages within us, we don't allow anyone the opportunity to love us for who we are.

Keep moving through the pain, my friend. You are strong enough to finish the race before you. During the most horrific miles, remember to take it one painful, agonizing step at a time. Don't stop moving forward, and the worst of it will be over before you know it.

You were made to do the impossible.

"No, I'm not giving up," I said, shrugging the medic's arm off my shoulders. I was determined to finish this race no matter what.

Miraculously, I managed to propel my body forward another tiny step, and then one more. I had no idea how I would make it, but I knew I had to. After a few more blocks, I inexplicably quickened my pace to a jog and locked eyes with a cheerful woman beside me.

"I'm really struggling. Could you talk to me for a few minutes?" I said.

I quickly learned about my new friend, Jeanie. A spunky mom of three, she was running her seventh marathon like a champ.

"Don't stop to walk," she proclaimed. "Just keep moving and you'll be done before you know it."

She talked to me about her son's crazy girlfriend and the intervention they staged for their Cheeto-addicted black lab. Her uplifting, brightly colored headband and unyielding confidence rubbed off on my failing body. She reached into her pocket and handed me a handful of gummy bears.

"My secret weapon," she said with a wide grin.

With enough encouragement to help me endure another mile, Jeanie continued on her journey. I had just enough momentum to believe I could actually reach the finish line.

"*Sam. Saaaaaaam!*" a rambunctious group shrieked at mile twenty-four.

Searching the crowd, I was shocked to see a group of my friends from church with my mentee, Ethan, who never told me they were coming. I wasn't alone in this impossible moment. From the sidewalk next to the road, they jogged alongside me for the entire homestretch and made jokes about feeling tired from our "long" run.

With my newfound company, before I knew it I was surrounded by the historic mansions of Summit Avenue in downtown St. Paul. I looked down the monstrous hill in front of me and beheld the finish line a half mile below. Thousands of people cheered every finisher, and an orchestra of cowbells cued just enough adrenaline to muster one tiny morsel of remaining strength.

From high ladders, cameras flashed as my feet pounded step after step. The world slipped into slow motion. I pointed one hand to the sky and hobbled under the checkered banner.

I had made it.

I had survived.

It was finished.

"Sam Eaton, 4:41:26," the announcer's deep voice bellowed from speakers two stories above.

Four hours, forty-one minutes, and twenty-six seconds of willing my body to that spot. Hundreds of runners, wrapped in shiny paper blankets, huddled on the ground. The scene looked more like a war triage site than the congratulatory party I'd imagined. A large, jolly man placed a finisher's medal around my neck, and I was ushered in line to have my photo taken against a colorful background. I raised my medal in celebration. "It was the hardest thing I've ever done," I told my fan club.

No one said, "You run like a girl."

They all said, "You were amazing."

No one said, "You aren't athletic."
They all said, "That was so inspiring."

No one said, "You should have given up."
They all said, "Great time for your first marathon."

After a few more minutes, I turned to Ethan and said, "If you ever hear me say the word *marathon* again, slap me in the face." To his complete elation, Ethan has slapped me hundreds of times and continues to slap me to this very day. But even a regular slap to the face can be a nice reminder that—no matter what life throws our way—we can do the impossible.

CHAPTER 18

YOU WERE MADE TO BELONG

AGE 27

AFTER RINGING THE UPPER-MIDDLE-CLASS DOORBELL, I shifted my weight, scanned the extravagant autumn décor, and wondered if Joanna Gaines had flown in to design it. An intricately carved pumpkin staring up at me judged my low-end jeans and store-bought guacamole. Behind a brightly colored accent door, a room full of people who used to know me better than anyone else on the planet had gathered. Unfortunately, the passage of time and major life events had created a distance between us I promised would never happen.

While I'd learned so much about fighting depression since the suicide attempt, I'd also discovered my journey toward better mental health required significantly more time and energy than I anticipated. When my depression was steering the ship, I wasn't a very good friend. I didn't call people back and cancelled plans at the last minute. I missed important parties because, on a rare occasion, sometimes I still didn't have the energy to get out of bed. After another tough season, however, for four weeks in a row I experienced almost no major symptoms and started to feel like my former self again: clear minded, wide awake, and missing my people.

As the door swung open, a group of dogs rushed to greet me and scattered throughout the newly renovated main level. The open-concept floor plan contained white shiplap accent walls and an expansive flat-screen television. The smell of chili filled every corner. We all exchanged hugs like the family we had been. Then, in small circles spread throughout the house, deck, and yard, we caught up on jobs, vacations, house projects, and families. Outside, I grabbed a hard cider from the cooler while bean bags flew over my head toward the cornhole boards. I quieted the overly competitive Hulk within me, who begged to challenge and destroy every unworthy contender in my path, and sat in an Adirondack chair. I pressed the cold bottle to my lips and drifted in and out of friends' conversations. For so long, I had deeply loved these incredible people.

My mind flashed back to the time we forgot to dock the boat properly and had to chase it five cabins down. I remembered playing night games—when a board nail slid out and cleanly stuck in a friend's butt cheek. (He was fine once the EMTs chuckled and pulled it out.) I recalled the bliss of rushing to our friend's bonfire pit the second we were all back in our hometown. It felt so good to be back.

"Any new relationships on the horizon, Sam?" The mention of my name snapped me into reality.

I considered answering, "Pretty sure I had a first date with a distant relative of Ted Bundy last night." Instead I said, "Same as usual," the answer most people had come to expect from me. Then I enthusiastically offered, "I've been working a lot on writing a book." But my words hung in the air without any follow-up questions.

The container of emptied cans and bottles grew fuller, and the music changed from acoustic guitars to nostalgic party anthems from our golden years. After a few hours, we gathered in the kitchen and ate from heaping plates. Every few minutes bursts of laughter overflowed from the group.

Maybe this was the new beginning I'd desperately hoped for.

Maybe I still belonged here.

Everyone's conversation halted when a gregarious spouse came back from the bathroom and yelled, "So are we all going on that big sky trip again this year? I'm just gonna say it—best trip we've ever been on!" He wrapped his arms around two of the guys.

His wife shot him a look which I took to mean, *Don't talk about that, Sam wasn't invited,* but this guy who had married into our group was always a little tone-deaf.

Intentional or not, out came story after story about the great beer they'd had in Mexico and the cabin trips that no longer included me. The room exploded with life. Meanwhile, I tried to fade into the wall, wishing I were dead.

"Who's gonna bite the bullet and get that massive hot tub installed first?" a brunette hollered out.

"What's the name of that bartender we had?" the Vikings jersey asked.

"Carlos!" everyone except me shouted in unison.

I waited for anyone to say, "Sam, you totally have to come this year," or even acknowledge my existence, but nobody said anything. No longer a main character in this story, I'd become a twice-a-year guest star at best. My chest tightened and burned, and a silent funeral began within me.

Life had changed.

I had changed.

I no longer belonged.

My life can feel like walking through a relationship graveyard, with headstones of living people as far as the eye can see. If I didn't work so hard on my mental health, my brain would love to live there, overanalyzing and obsessing about every joyful memory turned nightmare. For many years, I unsuccessfully attempted to make everyone permanently stay—probably because my mom, my sister, and one amazing aunt were my only real family. But when you never expect to lose anyone, you've set yourself up for one hell of a heartbreak.

I don't know if there's anything more disheartening than sitting in a place where you used to—but no longer—belong. Part of me wanted to stuff my pain and small talk until the end of time, thankful anyone wanted to be around me at all. Yet the more I fought to be recklessly alive, the more I valued myself and recognized when others didn't. With the help of my counselor and what I'd learned about who God had created me to be, I began to stand up for myself, set boundaries around toxic people, assert my voice in relationships, and, most importantly, believe I was worth more than being anyone's afterthought.

> I could have spent my life sprinkling ill will like an evil fairy godfather.

> I could have blamed others and never owned my part in the breakdown.

> I could have let the past consume and destroy the beautiful future waiting for me.

But God says if anyone starts following Jesus, the old is gone and the new has come.[19] I like that. At any point we can choose to start over and find ways to be more fully alive. For some this is instantaneous. (I mean, I don't know anyone like that, but good for you if it was.) Others, like me, find a little more freedom from the past one day at a time.

I hope you walk away from any place that keeps you from becoming the best version of yourself.

I hope you thank the people who have left and wish them well.

I hope you work so hard on yourself that people notice how much you've changed.

You are worth so much more than sitting on the outside looking in. You are too full of life to be half-loved. You were made to belong.

Closing the front door behind me, I began to mourn unexpectedly losing my people. Intense feelings of failure for letting the friendships die swept through me, as well as shame for no longer being wanted by the humans I never dreamed would cast me out. I glanced back through the glass window and saw the people that were once my family smiling and roaring with laughter.

As I drove away, I realized we weren't ever going back to the people we used to be.

Once safely home, I walked up the half-flight of stairs to the living room and collapsed onto the carpet. More than half of my photo wall contained pictures of these people who were now just people I used to know.

I released a painful breath and ached from the unexpected change of events. The new start I'd hoped for had sharply turned into the last page of a beautiful chapter I never wanted to end. Finally, I accepted the hardest truth of all—it was time to let go. Sometimes we have to walk away from a place that hurts more than it helps. Sometimes we have to move on and find a new place to belong.

CHAPTER 19

YOU WERE MADE TO MAKE A DIFFERENCE

AGE 27

THE WAILS OF CRYING babies filled the atmosphere like a symphony of despair. We, the outnumbered volunteers present at Mother Teresa's Clinic and Orphanage in Port-au-Prince, Haiti, were trying to console as many of our little friends as possible. Despite our best efforts and our game that involved earning points for bodily fluids on any piece of clothing (one point for urine, two points for poo, three points for vomit, and four points for diarrhea), our morning felt like an unbeatable game of baby whack-a-mole—using food and love instead of a hammer, of course.

My boots found their way to Haiti as a leader for fifteen high school kids from my church. Most of them were experiencing the world's extreme poverty for the first time, and I was becoming more obsessed with going to extremes in order to help people. We primarily served at a home for kids with special needs, but each morning the teens rotated through different volunteer opportunities. I—the only twenty-seven-year-old single guy with zero kids of my own—was selected to lead a small handful of students each day to a local clinic for sick or abandoned babies.

On my first day at Mama T's, my eyes widened as I entered a dusty stone room filled past capacity with over fifty cribs. Babies needed to be individually picked up, changed, and fed before they could go play. Some of the little people sat quiet and content, others slept through the cacophony of chaos, while the rest roared like lions in the jungle vying to be at the top of the orphanage food chain. Above the yelling, one screamer out-lunged them all. I followed the voice to the back, where a small fire-pistol of a child growled at me and grimaced with a what-the-heck-do-you-want look. I reached out my hands, imagining she would immediately embrace this tall, skinny Minnesotan. Instead, she whacked me in the jaw.

I stood by her crib, gently attempting to calm the lioness. She swung again. Her screams intensified to the decibel level of a fire alarm, so I looked around for a less abusive toddler. When I turned away from her, she exhaled, apparently resigned to the horrible reality that I was her only option for freedom. She reached out her hands for me to pick her up.

From that moment on, Cadet—a rambunctious bully of a girl—consistently attacked me, yet rarely left my side. Even though her poop smelled worse than any odor in the history of humanity, and she regularly pulled my armpit hair so hard I'd scream out in agony, an indescribable love that defied all logic (and safety) took root in my wiry frame.

Cadet had the entire world stacked against her. She lived in the poorest country of the Western Hemisphere and was sick—without any family to care for her. Despite my better judgment, I committed to spending the week doing my best to love the loudest and most unlovable child I'd ever met. Holding her five tiny fingers and slowly feeding her bite after bite of beef stew, I realized how much of my life I had wasted on things that didn't matter.

One afternoon, as the sun challenged my SPF-75 sunscreen to a duel, I unwrapped my guitar and lifted up a worship melody into the polluted air around me. My sweaty fingers moved through the chords they had played a million times.

Immediately, Cadet ran out from the corner and wiggled her way into my lap. The song barely continued as she palmed the strings and pushed my hands out of the way. As I struggled to make it through the second verse, a group jumped up and danced around, and somehow in a foreign country with a child I looked nothing like in my lap, the world felt a little more whole.

I wish every person were required to go serve at Mother Teresa's. To get to share a meal and dance with strangers at a hut in Zimbabwe. To have the honor of eating dinner with my homeless friend, Bill. Not because these people need us to save them, but because we need them to save us.

Maybe life has nothing to do with how happy you can make yourself, but how alive you can decide to become. There's a reason Jesus is the greatest example of how to be recklessly alive: He was relentless about making a difference and focusing on what matters most. He spent His time connecting with people, investing in others, taking care of Himself, listening to God, and choosing to love.

We are obsessed with stalking wealthy celebrities, lifting them up as the model everyone should aspire to be. I wonder if we lose so many famous people to addiction, crime, mental health, and suicide because they are burdened with our expectations to be the happiest people on earth. Happiness, however, is an emotion that comes and goes—a mirage no one can ever infinitely sustain. You can spend your whole life focusing on yourself, or you can chase a life that is fully and recklessly alive. You can't have both.

I hope you're brave enough to focus on what matters most.

I hope you're courageous enough to fight complacency and get your hands dirty.

I hope you finally realize that your life was never about you.

You were made to make a difference.

———

On the last day of my week at the orphanage, I walked into the room filled with wall-to-wall cribs. There, in the back, stood a screaming toddler with reddened eyes and a tear-soaked face. I hurried to Cadet. She immediately lifted her hands. After I placed my arms around her, she snuggled her face into my chest, fell silent, and smiled.

I held on to each precious moment that day, wishing time would stand still. I wondered what it would take to adopt her and bring her home with me. Even though sweat moistened every crevice of my body and bug bites itched every inch of my skin, a deep love for this incredible little being in my arms overtook me unlike anything I'd ever experienced. I hugged her tight again, and she pressed her nose to my nose.

Even though she didn't speak English, words from my past came pouring out of me.

"Everything will be alright," I said, this orphanage her version of my day in the woods.

"I know life can be scary. I know what it feels like to have a dad who can't or won't care for you. I know your life might seem impossible, but you are so freaking loved."

At the sound of the lunch bell, our signal to depart, Cadet fiercely wrapped her arms around my leg and refused to budge. I scooped her up one last time. She rested her head on my shoulder, and I rubbed her back. Then I kissed the top of her dirty head and lingered, trying to delay the inevitable.

"Sam, we have to go," someone from my group yelled into the room.

One of the nuns from the orphanage came in, thanking and pushing out all the volunteers until I was the only one left.

I gently placed Cadet back in her crib. She stared up at me with big brown eyes before looking away as if we both knew this was goodbye.

"You're a fighter, Cadet. You're gonna make it." I fought every instinct to pick her up and never let go.

PART FOUR

CHAPTER 20

YOU WERE MADE TO BE RECKLESSLY ALIVE

AGE 28

"TAKE SEVEN. SAM, RELAX and tell your story. *Action!*"

No part of me wanted to tell the world about the day I'd attempted to end my life. Nevertheless, there I was in the middle of an abandoned parking lot outside the 1910 Grain Belt Warehouse in northeast Minneapolis. The historic brick background, combined with long-deserted railroad ties, set the opening scene for my first suicide-prevention video.

A videographer hung out the open back end of a red Chrysler minivan. As it crept toward me in reverse, gravel crinkled beneath the tires. I tied my running shoes as the script directed and mentally coached my hands to stop shaking. Rising from the ground, I looked into the camera.

"Every 12.3 minutes someone in the U.S. commits suicide, and I was almost one of them. I knew the pain deep in my heart would never—" I froze, threw my hands up, and marched out of the shot.

"Cut!" Kari called from the van.

"I can't do this!" I yelled, rubbing my eyes with my sweaty palms.

Katrina emerged from the driver's seat. "Sam, just look at the camera and tell your story. We don't care what the script says. We simply want to hear what happened that day. You lived it. Now tell us."

She paused. Then she softly said, "Release the script. Embrace the story."

My lines were beyond memorized; however, I had drastically miscalculated the amount of courage this moment required. Despite Katrina's encouragement, I alternated between cycles of nausea and waves of angry tears as I struggled to internalize her advice.

During the preceding year, the school district where I taught had lost a student, a teacher, and a principal to suicide. When I opened up my email one morning, another message from the counseling staff jumped off the screen. *Sweet Jesus, no. We've lost another one.*

After scanning the tragic words, I dropped to the floor. I tried to shut out the magnitude of grief. My head sunk between my knees. Was there nothing we could do to stop this silent epidemic? The same nudge that had sent me to Africa, pushed me to say hello to Bill, and urged me to do something following the three previous community suicides came back stronger than ever.

I wonder if my story could help someone decide to stay?

I glanced at the clock. In less than thirty minutes, high-energy students expecting their weekly music lesson would fill my classroom. Nobody prepares you for just how hard teaching can be.

Unable to shake the ache to help, I decided—for the first time since age thirteen—to not get a summer job. It was an insanely uncharacteristic move considering, while I had made progress on student loans, I was far from free. The voice of common sense pandered to my doubts: *Work more, not less.* The nudge, however, could no longer be ignored. I trusted God would financially provide if I dedicated my summer to starting Recklessly Alive, a suicide-prevention organization aimed at a world with zero deaths from suicide.

In June, I stood in front of a microphone at the intermission of a songwriter friend's backyard show. A tiny crowd listened from lawn chairs while I shared statistics about depression and the heavily abridged story of my suicide attempt. Shaken, I left the stage—convinced I had made a terrible mistake—when a woman I'd never met ambushed me, squeezed her arms around my back, and sobbed into my shoulder for the next ten minutes.

"Thank you," she said over and over. "Thank you."

"Take eight!" Kari hollered.

I begged God to find someone else—anyone else—to be the spokesperson for this new organization I had founded. There had to be someone more popular, attractive, and articulate to be the face of this movement. What would people say when they learned the truth about me? How would my friends and family respond?

Pretending to tie my shoe, I knelt on the ground and fought to silence my calamitous brain. Thirty seconds into my lines, I stumbled again.

"Cut!" Kari yelled.

———

Sacrificing ourselves for the sake of others isn't exactly the backbone of most church cultures I've experienced. It's never the "pure joy" some Christians claim it to be from their movie theater seats while double fisting their pumpkin-spice lattes. But the reckless decision to love someone else no matter the cost is the kind of story Jesus invites all of us into.

Being recklessly alive isn't a nirvana-like state we achieve and enjoy until we take our last breath. Rather, it's a million little decisions we make.

To let life pass us by—or live it to the fullest.

To make ourselves happy—or discover true fulfillment in loving others.

To bury our deepest wounds—or get the help we deserve.

To hide all of our weaknesses—or use them to glorify God.

This is the craziest part of my story. When I tried to save my life through the comforts, wealth, and self-indulgence the world preaches, I wanted to die. But when I decided to lose my old way of life and try to live more like Jesus, I was finally saved.[20]

Choosing to go all in with God didn't instantly cure my mental illness. Fighting depression continues to be an ongoing mental, physical, and spiritual journey. Quite often, I'd rather hide than chase the waterfall moments God has planned for me. Some days I find myself trapped in the stupid dark room again, clawing at the door. Some days I still wake up thinking maybe I don't want to be alive. And that's real life. We fall and muster up enough strength to rise one more time.

If you're wondering if God is real, look at my story. Then look around. Living, breathing miracles are all around us. Becoming recklessly alive—after being two seconds away from completing suicide—is what He can do in anyone's life. He brings people back from the dead. It's His specialty.

"Every 12.8 minutes, someone in the U.S. commits suicide, and I was almost one of them," my voice boomed. The finished video played to a packed crowd in an enormous high school gym a year after its release.

"Choose to stay. Choose to tell someone about the pain deep in your heart. Choose to believe that today is not the end but a new beginning. Choose to run as fast as you can toward your big dreams—because they can happen. Choose to know deep in your heart that you truly matter, and you are truly loved. We need you here. Choose to live."

As the video faded to black, I slowly walked on stage. I paused, then spoke into the microphone.

"No part of me wanted to make that video. No part of me wants to be on this stage telling you about the worst day of my life." My body started to sweat. I already felt emotionally drained from the thought of baring my soul.

Nevertheless, for forty minutes I somehow managed to share the hardest parts of my story—lightened with my signature brand of humor—with nearly a thousand strangers. A screen presented a picture of me as a kid while I talked about my dad leaving home. The screen displayed one of the last photos taken of me before the attempt as I talked about writing goodbye letters. The screen turned black when I told the audience about counting backward from ten. Then I clicked a Bible verse onto the screen—one that perfectly described my life:

> It stands to reason, doesn't it, that if the alive-and-present God who raised Jesus from the dead moves into your life, he'll do the same thing in you that he did in Jesus, bringing you alive to himself? When

God lives and breathes in you (and he does, as surely as he did in Jesus), you are delivered from that dead life. With His Spirit living in you, your body will be as alive as Christ's![21]

Nearing the end of my talk, I showed a dozen photos of incredible moments I would have missed. Photos of Zimbabwe and Haiti. Photos of finishing the marathon. Photos of semiannual cabin trips with my new friends. Photos of graduating with my master's degree—and the day I finally paid off every dollar of my student-loan debt. Photos of my awesome mom, my wonderful sister and her husband, and my beautiful niece and nephew.

"I want to ask you one final question. Have you really given life everything you've got? Because whatever you are going through, I promise there is so much help and so much hope. Choose to stay. Choose to live. Thank you."

A small group near the stage erupted to their feet, and within seconds everyone in the gym rose for a standing ovation. Soon the emcee entered the stage, and I exited into the lobby. Within minutes a line of people waiting to talk with me had formed down the hall.

"I lost my son four years ago," said one woman. Her voice choked up. "I can't thank you enough for doing what you're doing."

"We brought an entire vanload from our church," a group of young adults said. "We drove four hours to come hear you speak."

"You've completely inspired me," a teenage girl exclaimed as she gave me a giant hug. "I want to share my story, too, and do what you're doing."

Suicide is never the answer, my friend. There's a better way to stop the piercing pain in your heart. You can find your purpose and heal the darkness inside. God really can use all things for good—including the worst days of your life.[22]

I can't promise your journey will be easy, or horrible things won't happen to you. But I can promise there is always a way forward—even when everything feels impossible. There are adventures ahead that are better than you can imagine and people in the world who need to hear your story. You're not alone. We're in this together.

Now, go give life everything you've got. Your recklessly alive life is out there—and it's waiting for you.

NOTES

1   Jeremiah 1:5
2   Philippians 4:7
3   Jeremiah 1:5
4   Jeremiah 31:3
5   Genesis 1:27
6   1 Samuel 16:7
7   Deuteronomy 31:6
8   2 Corinthians 5:17
9   Psalm 139:14
10   Matthew 19:26
11   John 8:12
12   John 10:10
13   Psalm 103:12
14   Jeremiah 29:11
15   John 3:16
16   John 10:10
17   Ephesians 2:3 (MESSAGE)
18   Matthew 19:26
19   2 Corinthians 5:17
20   Luke 9:24
21   Romans 8:11 (MESSAGE)
22   Romans 8:28

ACKNOWLEDGMENTS

Mom — Thank you for all the sacrifices you have made to give me an incredible life. I love you forever.

Beth — I can never thank you enough for your unyielding dedication to this project. You have left an unmeasurable impact on my life and I couldn't be more thankful for your editing, encouragement, and friendship.

Jason, Varonnica, and Grace from Creative Edge — Thank you for your work on the cover and interior design. You took my vision and blew it out of the water.

Sami — Thank you for being all in for me and Recklessly Alive. The amount of love you have for people is unmatched in anyone I've ever met.

Bryan — Thank you for being one of the first men to stay in my life. You have consistently stood by me and lifted me up when I wanted to give up on myself.

Rob — Thank you for being such a good friend and mentor to me. You are an incredible example of Jesus. You have helped me so many times when I've wanted to give up on God.

Marcia and Catherine - Thank you immensely for your incredible editing and guidance through the final stages of this project.

My friends and supporters – Seven years ago I started pursuing this dream of having a book published. Through every up and down, I have been beyond blessed by your continued love and encouragement. I have thought many times about deleting Recklessly Alive, but you have all kept me going. Thank you.

Recklessly Alive is a faith-based mental wellness organization sprinting toward a world with zero deaths from suicide. It exists to create a spiritual movement that empowers others to be fully alive in Christ through engaging online content, helpful resources, and life-changing events. Believing every life is valuable to God, Recklessly Alive will never stop leaving the ninety-nine to find the one who feels lost, hopeless, and alone.

RecklesslyAlive.com | @RecklesslyAlive

ABOUT THE AUTHOR

Sam Eaton was born in Minneapolis, Minnesota, where he learned to let all drivers merge with a smile. He is a powerful voice for his generation as an innovative ministry leader and sought-after communicator. In 2016, after losing five people to suicide in his hometown, he founded Recklessly Alive (recklesslyalive.com), an organization sprinting toward a world with zero deaths from suicide. He speaks throughout the U.S. and encourages everyone he meets to chase a life that is fully and recklessly alive. Sam has a master's degree in educational leadership and has taught music in the public schools for over ten years. He is on a lifelong quest to love God, love people, expand his vinyl record collection, and try every flavor of Oreos.

Made in the USA
Las Vegas, NV
18 July 2022

51423888R10105